The YOSEMITE HANDBOOK

An Insider's Guide to the Park

As related by
Bruinhilda

By Susan and Phil Frank

Pomegranate

SAN FRANCISCO

Published by Pomegranate
Box 6099, Rohnert Park, CA 94927

Pomegranate Europe Ltd.
Fullbridge House, Fullbridge
Maldon, Essex CM9 4LE, England

As the events of 1997 have shown us, everything is in a process of constant
change in and around Yosemite. For that reason, although we made our best
efforts to retrieve the most up-to-date information as possible at press time, we
cannot guarantee the accuracy or completeness of the contents of this book. The
publisher and author assume no legal responsibility for the effects of inclusion or
exclusion of any premises or services, commercial or otherwise, from this book.
The names of businesses are provided as a service to readers and not as a recom-
mendation or guarantee.

Library of Congress Cataloging-in-Publication Data

Frank, Susan, 1948–
        The Yosemite handbook : an insider's guide to the park, as
    related by Bruinhilda / by Susan and Phil Frank.
             p. cm.
    Includes bibliographical references and index.
    ISBN 0-7649-0616-X (pb : alk. paper)
        1. Yosemite National Park (Calif.)—Guidebooks. I. Frank, Phil.
II. Title.
F868.Y6F73   1998
917.94′470453—dc21   97-43405
                                                     CIP

Pomegranate Catalog No. A920
ISBN 0-7649-0616-X

Interior design by Shannon Lemme
Printed in USA
07 06 05 04 03 02 01 00 99 98 10 9 8 7 6 5 4 3 2 1

Contents

Acknowledgments

We wish to thank Josh Englander for his invaluable help in developing and editing the manuscript; Keith Walklet of Yosemite Concession Services Corporation for his ongoing advice and support; Steven P. Medley and the Yosemite Association for their generous assistance with research and resource materials; Annie Malley of the Bio-diversity Resource Center, California Academy of Sciences, for her technical expertise; the National Park Service staff at Yosemite, especially Dean Shenk for his careful review of the manuscript, and Craig Bates, Bruce Brossman, Christine Cowles, Norma Craig, Linda Eade, Scott Gediman, Oly Olsen, Jim Snyder, Kendell Thompson, and Steve Thompson for their technical assistance and help in making this guidebook as accurate as possible.

S. F. and P. F.

Introduction

Your guide through this handbook will be Bruinhilda, the matriarch of a bear clan from "Farley," Phil Frank's daily cartoon strip that runs in the *San Francisco Chronicle*. Although Bruinhilda and her cartoon bear friends make their home in the San Francisco Bay Area, their most popular antics have taken place during their frequent trips to the Yosemite area. We thought she would be the most qualified to answer your questions!

The question-and-answer format of this book originally came from "100+ Common Visitor Questions & Answers," a document that the National Park Service's Division of Interpretation at Yosemite National Park prepared and revised in April 1995 to help park rangers and interpretive staff at Yosemite get quickly oriented.

Working from that idea, we have put together many of those same questions plus lots of others to help visitors get quickly oriented. We hope the book will add to your enjoyment of this beautiful park.

Welcome to Yosemite National Park. My name's Hilda... Bruinhilda to be exact. I'll be your guide, along with my pals here, to show you around.
Remember... we're just cartoons. The real animals of Yosemite are wild creatures- not cute cartoons!
Don't feed or try to approach them, but **do** enjoy your visit!

I.
Getting
there

YOSEMITE
OR BUST!

Where is Yosemite?

On the eastern side of California, where mountains reach the sky and trees outnumber people, Yosemite sits atop the Sierra Nevada, spilling down both sides of the range to about thirty miles from the Nevada border and 225 miles from the Pacific Ocean. We're closer to Oregon than Mexico, so if you imagined California as a bear standing up, we're about at its left elbow.

Here are some road mileage figures and approximate driving times to Yosemite Valley to help you plan your trip (based on 50 MPH and 35 MPH inside the park):

Via Highway 41
From Los Angeles	313 miles (6.25 hours)
From Bakersfield	201 miles (4.25 hours)
From Fresno	94 miles (2.5 hours)
From Oakhurst	50 miles (1.5 hour)
From Fish Camp	37 miles (1 hour)

Via Highway 140
From San Francisco	219 miles (4.5 hours)
From Sacramento	199 miles (4 hours)
From Stockton	140 miles (3.5 hours)
From Merced	81 miles (2 hours)
From Mariposa	43 miles (1.25 hours)
From El Portal	14 miles (30 minutes)

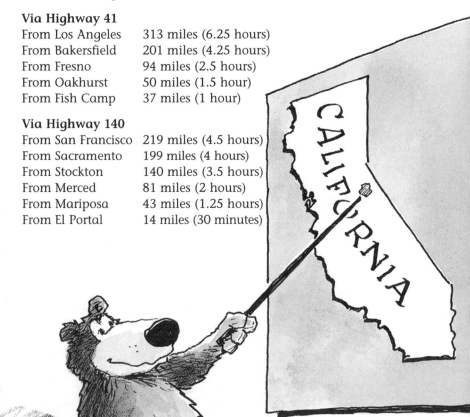

Via Highway 120 from the west

From San Francisco	195 miles (4.5 hours)
From Sacramento	176 miles (4 hours)
From Stockton	127 miles (3 hours)
From Manteca	117 miles (2.75 hours)
From Oakdale	96 miles (2.25 hours)
From Sonora	60 miles (2 hours)
From Groveland	49 miles (1.5 hours)

Via Highway 120 from the east

From Las Vegas	460 miles (8 hours)
From Los Angeles	409 miles (9 hours)
From Reno	218 miles (5 hours)
From Lake Tahoe	190 miles (4.5 hours)
From Carson City	188 miles (4.5 hours)
From Bishop	146 miles (3.5 hours)
From Mammoth Lakes	106 miles (2.5 hours)
From Lee Vining	74 miles (2 hours)

How do we get there?

Depending on time and money, you can get to Yosemite by car, bus, train or plane.

Drivers have a choice of four roads to the park. From the south, Highway 41 runs from Fresno through Oakhurst and Fish Camp to the South Entrance, where you'll find the Mariposa Grove of giant sequoias and the Wawona Hotel (2.5 hours from Fresno).

From the west, Highway 140 rolls along the river through Merced, Cathey's Valley, Mariposa, and El Portal to the famous Arch Entrance (approximately two hours from Merced). From here, it's an easy uphill drive along the river into the valley.

Highway 120 from the northwest wanders through Manteca, Oakdale, Moccasin, Groveland, and Buck Meadows, winding up at the Big Oak Flat Entrance (a little less than 3 hours from Manteca). This steep descent into the valley provides spectacular vistas.

Starting from the east, your only access is through Lee Vining near Mono Lake and over California's highest auto route: the 9,945-foot Tioga Pass, which leads into the park's high country wilderness (close to 2 hours from Lee Vining). This section is always closed in winter. For recorded road and weather information, call (209) 372-0200.

Of the hundreds of bus companies that come to Yosemite, I'll mention just a few to give you an idea of the range of services available. You can catch a daily VIA bus from either the AMTRAK or Greyhound stations in Merced or at the airport in Fresno. VIA offers a Yosemite-in-a-Day tour, which includes transportation, a boxed lunch, and a two-hour Yosemite Valley tram tour. Call (800) 369-PARK (in California) or (209) 384-1315.

From northern California, one-day bus excursions with Tower Tours depart from San Francisco. Call (800) 587-9484. For a little more

Kibble Lake
Flora Lake
Lake Eleanor
Price Peak
△ 10,716 ft.
Rock Island Lake
Quarry Peak
11,161 ft.

Yosemite

Hetch Hetchy Reservoir
Grand Canyon of the Tuolumne
Glen Aulin High Camp
Tuolumne Meadows
120

MATHER

White Wolf Lodge
May Lake High Camp

120

Tuolumne Grove BIG TREES
TIOGA ROAD
Crane Flat

Sunrise High Camp

Tuolumne Meadows Lodge and High Camp

Vogelsang High Camp

HALF DOME

△ Mt. Lyell 13,114 ft.

Merced Lake High Camp

El Portal
YOSEMITE VALLEY
GLACIER POINT
Mt. Clark 11,522 ft.

140
MERCED
Chinquapin
Badger Pass Ski Area

WAWONA
Mariposa Grove Big Trees

41
TO FRESNO AND ROUTE 99

5

luxury, California Parlor Car of San Francisco offers one-, two-, or three-day tours with overnight stays at the Yosemite Lodge or Ahwahnee hotel, one lunch, and a two-hour valley tram tour. Call (415) 474-7500. Or, for a bus of your very own, call Preferred Charters in Santa Rosa at (707) 585-9110.

With daily AMTRAK train service from Oakland/Emeryville to Merced, and from Los Angeles and San Diego to Fresno and Merced, you can ride some of the way by rail. For train and bus reservations, call (209) 454-2080 or (800) 872-7245.

Birds can land anywhere in Yosemite, but you'll have to fly into one of the San Francisco Bay Area airports (San Francisco, Oakland, or San Jose) and drive 4.5 hours to the park, or into one of the southland airports (LAX, Orange County, Burbank, or Ontario) and drive 5.5 hours to the South Entrance. Closer to the park, you can take one of fourteen airlines to the Reno-Tahoe Airport, then drive 4.5 hours to the Tioga Pass Entrance. Landing in Fresno or Merced, you can drive 2 hours to the South Entrance. Call the airlines or a travel agent for more information.

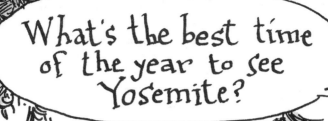

What's the best time of the year to see Yosemite?

As a year-round resident of the park, I can tell you that every season in Yosemite has something special to offer.

The blooming of spring is one of my favorite times, when fresh colors and the calls of wildlife emerge from the big freeze. Runoff from snowfall swells the rivers and creeks, giving visitors a thunderous display of our famous waterfalls. Best of all, there are fewer visitors in March and April, which means less of a crowd at the exhibits, restaurants, and stores. Since the park is still digging out from winter, some of our campgrounds and trails are not yet open, especially in the high country.

Summer is the season of more: more people, more activities, more campgrounds to choose from, and more services available from June through Labor Day. Most of the waterfalls dry up, but the rivers and lakes have better fishing. Backpackers, wilderness campers, and rock climbers love using the long, warm days of the season to tackle Yosemite's challenging landscape.

The fall leaves us with good weather, fewer people, and a chance to experience the slow withdrawal of nature into winter. From September to November, there's less daylight in which to see the colors of the trees and fields, which are glowing with the brightest colors of the year.

Winter's sleepy spell transforms the park into another world. It's time for visitors to trade in their hiking boots for skis and snowshoes, and experience Yosemite at its most serene. Some access roads close, but many of the park's facilities remain open, including four of the campgrounds: Upper Pines and Sunnyside in the valley as well as Hodgdon Meadow and Wawona.

Hmm...

7

How much does it cost to get in?

It's certainly cheaper than an amusement park, where the mountains are fake and the animals are usually people in costumes. As you enter one of the four park gates, you'll pay an entrance fee that's good for seven days, and the ranger will give you a map with basic park information and a free copy of the *Yosemite Guide*, the park newspaper with up-to-date listings and schedules for park activities. For educational fee waivers, call (209) 375-9527.

Private non-commercial vehicles $20
(valid for seven days)

Individuals arriving by bus, foot, bicycle, motorcycle, or horse $10
(valid for seven days)

Annual Yosemite Pass $40

Golden Eagle Pass $50
(good for all National Parks for one year from date of purchase)

Golden Age Pass $10
(a lifetime pass for all National Parks for U.S. citizens who are 62 and older)

Golden Access Pass . . . . .Free
(for blind or permanently disabled U.S. citizens or permanent residents)

Is the park always open to visitors?

The park is supposed to be open twenty-four hours a day, 365 days a year, but every once in a while Mother Nature decides to temporarily close the gates.

Though I slept through most of it, two and a half days of warm and heavy rains from January 1–3, 1997, brought the greatest flooding to hit Yosemite Valley in one hundred years and closed the valley completely for two and a half months. The rough winter runoff of 1995 created a heap of problems in spring and summer. In March, flooding and rock slides caused by winter runoff closed two main entrances and the high country trails; a couple of months later, we had a June snowstorm that dumped so much snow that the High Sierra Camps and roads outside Yosemite Valley had to be closed. In 1990 lightning storms started a series of fires that shut down the entire park for a week. For current twenty-four-hour information on park and road conditions, call (209) 372-0200.

It's not always Mother Nature's fault; sometimes it's just plain human nature that makes the park inaccessible. In 1995, there were so many visitors motoring around the park that it became impossible for anyone to drive into Yosemite Valley—seven weekends in a row!

For the first time in the park's history, Yosemite was closed to visitors twice in 1995 because of a government shutdown. During the Christmas season, all the hotels and visitor facilities were empty, so I didn't get any leftovers from the Bracebridge Dinner at the Ahwahnee, or hear the distant music coming from the traditional New Year's dance.

The park is open 365 days a year!

Nature permitting...

FACTS ABOUT YOSEMITE NATIONAL PARK

- Native Americans lived in Yosemite 4,000 years before the Gold Rush.

- First tourists arrived in Yosemite in 1855.

- John Muir first visited Yosemite in 1868.

- Yosemite National Park was established on October 1, 1890.

- David and Jenny Curry opened a small camp for tourists in Yosemite in 1899.

- The size of Yosemite is 748,542 acres or 1,169 square miles.

- 94 percent of the park is designated wilderness.

- Yosemite has:
  - 360 miles of paved roads
  - 800 miles of developed trails
  - 880 miles of rivers and streams

- Yosemite Valley is seven square miles.

- 75 to 80 percent of all visitors to Yosemite stay in the valley.

- Growth in Annual Visitors to Yosemite:

Year	Visitors
1855:	42
1899:	4,500
1922:	100,506
1940:	506,781
1954:	1,008,031
1986:	2,982,758
1991:	3,547,163
1996:	4,190,557

What services are available?

Most of the visitor facilities and services are in Yosemite Valley. That's probably why seventy-five to eighty percent of park visitors spend all their time in the valley. Here's what you'll find within its seven square miles: the Visitor Center, Ahwahnee hotel, Yosemite Lodge, Curry Village, Ansel Adams Gallery, Housekeeping Camp, a grocery store, deli, post office, repair garage, free shuttle service, medical clinic, a wilderness center, chapel, bicycle rentals, recycling center, campgrounds, ATM machine, cashier's office, public restrooms, showers, laundromat, a jail, and photocopy and fax machines in the hotels. Ah, yes—the great outdoors.

About twenty-five miles south of Yosemite is the historic community of Wawona. Here you'll find the Wawona Hotel, Pioneer Yosemite History Center, a grocery store, gas station, and nine-hole golf course. There's no shuttle or regular commercial bus service to this part of the park.

Fifty-five miles north of the valley lies most of Yosemite National Park; a good chunk of this portion is wilderness area. Most of the services in this part of the park can be found in and around Tuolumne Meadows, including the Visitor Center, four lodges (two lodges inside the park and two just outside its boundaries), two gas stations (Tuolumne Meadows and Crane Flat), a store and grill, post office, ranger station, wilderness permit station, restrooms, and countless miles of the best trails in the Sierra.

Hi. We're lost, hungry, need an ATM, a bathroom, gasoline, a room and we want to mail this postcard.

11

Who runs Yosemite?

The United States National Park Service (NPS), which is part of the Department of the Interior, makes the rules in Yosemite National Park. This means you won't see any highway patrol, sheriffs, or municipal firefighters during your visit.

But that doesn't mean we animals run the park. The NPS has plenty of people around who make sure things run smoothly. Park rangers handle law enforcement, traffic regulation, search and rescue, and other duties. Park interpreters provide all the educational walks, talks, and programs in the park. The people dressed in green pants, gray shirts, and dark green baseball caps are the park maintenance, fire, and resource management workers. All these people answer to the NPS administrators like the superintendent and chief ranger, who manage Yosemite from their park offices.

To help with all the lodging, food services, bus tours, horse rides, and most of the shops in the park, the NPS has a contract with a private concession company, but the NPS authorizes the prices and service rates. The Yosemite Park & Curry Company had the job for seventy years, until 1993, when the Yosemite Concession Services Corporation (YCS) took over with a fifteen-year contract.

YOU CAN CONTACT THE NPS AND YCS AT THE FOLLOWING ADDRESSES:

National Park Service
P.O. Box 577, Yosemite National Park, CA 95389
(209) 372-0200; (General park information; recorded)
(209) 372-0265; (NPS Public Information Office: weekdays, 9–12 and 1–5)

Yosemite Concession Services Corporation
5410 E. Home Avenue, Fresno, CA 93727
(209) 252-4848 (lodging reservations for YCS facilities)
(209) 372-1000 (Yosemite; automated information)

Where can we stay?

There are a total of 1,519 rooms within the park, ranging from basic to deluxe. To get the best place for your needs, reserve early by mailing to Central Reservations, Yosemite Concession Services, 5410 East Home, Fresno, CA 93727 (see the lodging reservation form in this book's "Quick Reference" section on page 149) or by calling (209) 252-4848.

If you want to stay in the valley, you had better reserve your lodging as far in advance as possible, which is one year and one day (366 days) before your arrival. This way, you'll probably get your first choice of rooms in Curry Village, Housekeeping Camp, Yosemite Lodge, and the Ahwahnee hotel. The same goes for other lodgings in the park, including the Wawona Hotel, White Wolf, and the Tuolumne Meadows Lodge in the summer.

The rates vary according to amenities offered. A basic tent cabin with cots, blankets and a bathroom nearby costs $42.50 a night, while a billowy bed at the Ahwahnee hotel runs over $200 (rates subject to change).

You can also bunk down at a place outside the park, where various lodges, hotels, and motels await. For more information, turn to the Lodging and Dining chapter on page 59. For camping and backpacking information, turn to page 73.

What should we bring?

I suppose you could bring just about anything, like a bowling ball or a lawnmower, but they're not going to do you much good here. What you should bring depends on your accommodations and activities of choice, but I can tell you some basic items that will make your trip more comfortable. For advice on special activities, turn to the corresponding sections of this book.

Our weather is generally predictable. From spring through fall we have warm days and cool nights, so remember to bring an extra layer of clothing for evenings. In the winter our temperatures average in the high forties and fifties in the valley, but the higher you go, the colder the air. A cotton sweatshirt and a pair of jeans won't be enough, but a wool sweater underneath a water-resistant shell is almost as good as my coat. Heat escapes from your head and hands, so pack a pair of gloves and a cap that covers your ears.

I've seen people in the park who are red as a radish and covered with bug bites, but you can save yourself the misery by bringing sunscreen and insect repellent. A first-aid kit is always a good idea, along with a pair of boots or sturdy sneakers for hiking, walking, and bicycling. Binoculars will help in spotting wildlife, and a camera will provide the proof that you were here. Once you're tucked away in your tent or cabin, it's always nice to have a good book and games to while the night away.

Can Fido come, too?

You can bring your pets with you as long as you follow some strict rules. Pets must be leashed at all times and are only allowed on paved roads and bike paths. They can't follow you on trails, in buildings, or in the back country, unless they're seeing-eye or hearing signal dogs, or Canine Companions for people with other disabilities.

We do have "pet camping areas." In the summer, you and your furry friends can pitch a tent at Upper Pines, Wawona, Bridalveil Creek, Hodgdon Meadow, Crane Flat, White Wolf, Yosemite Creek, and Tuolumne Meadows. In the winter, pets are allowed in three campgrounds: Upper Pines, Wawona, and Hodgdon Meadow.

These rules are made for good reason. Our delicate ecosystem isn't ready for the wild mountain Chihuahua or free-range Labrador. Just about any kind of pet could create problems for the park wildlife and their natural habitats, not to mention other visitors. The park rangers keep careful watch on these regulations, and they're not shy about handing out $50 to $100 citations to rule-breakers. There are no longer any kennel facilities for short-term boarding in Yosemite Valley.

- El Capitan (three thousand feet) is the tallest unbroken cliff in the world.

- The first climb of El Capitan's face was made in 1958.

- Yosemite Falls (over twenty-four hundred feet) is the highest free-falling waterfall in the United States, with Sentinel Fall (two thousand feet) a close second.

- High water measurements in Yosemite Valley:

23.45 ft.	January 2, 1997
21.52 ft.	December 23, 1955
16.96 ft.	December 23, 1964

- Yosemite's ten highest peaks:
  1. Mt. Lyell: 13,114 ft.
  2. Mt. Dana: 13,053 ft.
  3. Rodgers Peak: 12,978 ft.
  4. Mt. Maclure: 12,960 ft.
  5. Mt. Gibbs: 12,764 ft.
  6. Mt. Conness: 12,590 ft.
  7. Mt. Florence: 12,561 ft.
  8. Simmons Peak: 12,503 ft.
  9. Excelsior Mountain: 12,446 ft.
  10. Electra Peak: 12,442 ft.

II
Park Attractions:

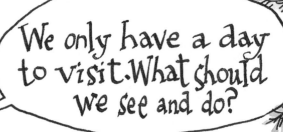

> We only have a day to visit. What should we see and do?

When long-time ranger Carl Sharsmith was asked this question, he replied, "Go out into that meadow, sit down, and cry." Well, I'd like to offer a few more suggestions. For starters, leave your car (follow signs to day-use parking at Curry Village) and take the shuttle bus around Yosemite Valley. The Valley Visitor Center will give you some good background information, then you can hike around the valley and see the real thing. Other one-day visitors might like to take a two-hour tram tour or a two-to-four-hour audio tour in their own car, followed by short excursions to some scenic lookouts. The tram tour runs every half hour in the summer and costs $16 for adults and $8.50 for children. Tickets are available from the tour desks at Yosemite Lodge, Curry Village, Yosemite Village, and the Ahwahnee hotel. The tram stops at all of these spots to pick up and drop off visitors. The audio tour tapes are available at the Valley Visitor Center.

SOME SURE-FIRE STOPS:

Yosemite Valley Visitor Center
Located in the Yosemite Village, the center offers tours and a video tailor-made for you one-dayers called "One Day in Yosemite."

Yosemite Museum
Next to the visitor center, the museum offers changing displays of famous Yosemite artwork. There's also a re-created Miwok Indian village, where you can take a self-guided walking tour.

Walk to Lower Yosemite Fall
From shuttle bus stop #7, you can walk a quarter mile to the base of Lower Yosemite Fall, one of our greatest sights (thirty-minute walk; see page 25).

Happy Isles Family Nature Center
Near shuttle stop #16 (summer only), the Nature Center has films, exhibits, and nature programs for kids during the summer. From here, you can walk less than a mile to Vernal Fall Bridge for the best view of the fall. If you have energy to burn, hike on along famous Mist Trail to the top of Vernal and Nevada falls (8.5 miles).

Walk to Mirror Lake
It's a half-mile to Mirror Lake from shuttle stop #17. The lake is filling with sediment, but it still has an awesome view of Half Dome. If you find a meadow instead of a lake, that means it's already completed its yearly late-fall transformation.

Mariposa Grove of the Big Trees
Yosemite's largest grove of giant sequoias is located near the South Entrance on Highway 41. During the summer, trams take you through the grove for a fee, or you can take the steep hike to the top. The grove's museum exhibits a natural history of the trees, including the amazing Grizzly Giant and the fallen Tunnel Tree (open summer only).

Spectacular Views of Yosemite
Just one hour's drive from the valley, Glacier Point offers a bird's eye view of the entire valley. Exhibits describe the geology of the park and identify major peaks (Glacier Point Road is closed in winter).

From the valley, follow road signs to Highway 41 toward Fresno, then turn left into the Bridalveil Fall parking lot, a ten- to fifteen-minute drive from the eastern end of Yosemite Valley. A short trail leads to the base of the fall, where water plunges 620 feet to the valley floor

Also from Highway 41, drive approximately three miles to the Tunnel View turnout. This is the historic panorama seen by Yosemite's first visitors 100 years ago (ten- to thirty-minute drive from the eastern end of Yosemite Valley).

Open in the summer only, the Tioga Road takes you through magical Tuolumne Meadows. Don't miss Olmstead Point looking out over Tenaya Lake and the back side of Half Dome.

What's the best way to get oriented?

Getting a feel for the park is like scooping honey from a beehive: no matter which hive you pick, it's going to be good (don't try this at home—unless you're a bear). I suggest leaving your car at the Curry Village day-use parking lot and taking a free shuttle around Yosemite Valley, the heart of the park.

The Yosemite Valley Visitor Center (shuttle stop #3, #6, or #9) is a great place to get your bearings. You can talk to rangers, view the Yosemite slide show and videos, browse the bookstore, and pick up a copy of the *Yosemite Guide* newspaper for the latest information on park activities.

From there on it's up to you. You can ride the free shuttle to one or all of the nineteen stops along the route (buses run every twenty minutes in winter and every few minutes in the summer), or take a two-hour tram tour of all the valley's famous sights. Another choice is the Yosemite Valley audio tour, which you can pick up for $9.95 at the Visitor Center. This two- to four-hour tour guides you to ten sites in the valley, describing the park's scenery, geology, and history along the way.

Hikers and backpackers won't want to miss the new Wilderness Center, just east of the Visitor Center on the pedestrian mall. There's plenty of information on the park's backcountry, complete with educational exhibits and a helpful trip-planning section. This is also the place to get your free wilderness permits or make camping reservations up to twenty-four weeks in advance (see page 163).

How was the Valley formed?

Would you believe the entire park was once beneath the sea? That's when the story begins, about 470 million years ago.

Due to a number of geologic processes—including the shifting of the earth's tectonic plates—and moisture and heat deep under the ocean floor, rock melted and the Sierra Nevada mountain range began to rise about one hundred million years ago.

The molten masses cooled to granite rock, leaving a broad valley of rolling hills with a river now known as the Merced River running through it. Meanwhile, further uplift carved into the river and hills, cutting into the once-broad valley, beginning its transformation into a steep canyon rimmed by granite peaks.

More than one million years ago, nature got its own Michelangelo—the Ice Age. Ice filled the entire region, and like a sculptor chiseling away at a huge block of marble, the ice began carving the land into what it is today: steep cliffs, rounded domes, and a lush valley floor. When the last glaciers melted away twenty thousand years ago, they left behind a lake in the valley. Today you can roam around the forests and meadows that have taken its place.

BROAD VALLEY STAGE. About twenty-five million years ago Yosemite Valley was a rolling landscape of low hills and a broad valley with the Merced River meandering through it. El Capitan rose in gentle curves to a height of only 900 feet, and Half Dome could be seen as an irregular form 500 feet above the lay of the land. There were no dramatic cliffs or waterfalls.

CANYON STAGE. From ten to two million years ago great uplifts and large water runoffs caused the Merced River to cut into the valley floor, forging a deep, walled canyon with a fast-moving river. The Yosemite uplands area rose several thousand feet above the river but had not yet acquired the sharp-edged rims that we see today.

GLACIAL STAGE. More than one million years ago the Ice Age brought glaciers from the High Sierra down through Yosemite Valley, widening its river canyon, steepening its walls and rims, and polishing its domes and towers. As the last glacier left, it cut back the rough walls of the deep river canyon, widening the valley and revealing sheer, smooth cliffs and its spectacular waterfalls.

LAKE STAGE. After each glacier, the floor of the valley was covered by a lake. The last glacier left ancient Lake Yosemite, which was probably only about twenty-five feet deep. Since then the lake basin has filled with earth, and in its place are the meadows and forests that park visitors enjoy today.

What happened to the other half of Half Dome?

Some people see our famous landmark as half empty, others think of it as half full. I just see it as a big rock reaching to the sky.

It seems I might be closest to the truth. According to geologists, it never was a complete dome. Millions of years have chipped away just a small portion of the granite mountain. The latest guess is that only twenty percent of Half Dome's size has been worn away over the ages.

So where did that portion go? During the Ice Age more than one million years ago, glaciers filled nearly the entire valley, leaving only the top seven hundred feet of Half Dome's forty-eight-hundred-foot height above ice. The melting glaciers likely washed away small portions of Half Dome to the valley floor, leaving them buried in the earth. Other pieces may have been swept away by flood waters to places as far away as the San Joaquin Valley.

Over time, Half Dome will probably continue to be whittled by the same forces and carried to faraway places, including the Pacific Ocean.

What's the best way to see the waterfalls?

Although we have thirteen falls in the park, only four are accessible by trail. During spring's snowmelt, the waterfalls come crashing down, until summer, when most of these great rushes have slowed to a trickle or completely dried up. If you're a waterfall hunter, the best month to catch your prey is usually May.

Yosemite Falls

Upper and Lower Yosemite Falls, with a cascade between them, add up to be the highest waterfall in North America, over twenty-four hundred feet. One of the best views of this year-round waterfall is seen in spring. Looking up from the valley as the early afternoon sun casts shadows on the falls, you'll see jets of water shoot out clearly from the granite cliffs.

There are a few ways to get to the Yosemite Falls trailhead. You can take the shuttle from the Valley Visitor Center to stop #7 at the Yosemite Falls parking area and walk ten minutes to the base of the falls. You can also walk down the bicycle path from the Visitor Center. Following the "park exits" signs by car is an option, but in the summer you'll need some luck finding a parking space.

Bridalveil Fall

Plummeting 620 feet down the west end of the valley, Bridalveil Fall is famous for its veil of mist, best seen around 1 p.m., when it's lit by direct sunlight. Bridalveil is another of our all-season falls, dropping from a "hanging valley" just behind the cliff top.

Off Highway 41 toward Fresno, the Bridalveil parking lot is the start of a fifteen-minute walk to the base of the falls. Don't forget: from Yosemite Valley there are two signed turns for Highway 41, and you must take them both.

Lower Yosemite Fall→

25

Vernal and Nevada Falls

Flowing down Yosemite's "Giant Staircase," the Merced River takes two big drops down to the valley below: Vernal Fall's 317-foot drop and Nevada Fall's 594-foot giant plunge.

The view of Vernal Fall from Happy Isles, which the Miwok called the "Meeting of the Waters," is best seen in the morning. If you walk up the trail from the Nature Center around 10 a.m., you just might see the sunlight transform the plunging water into falling jewels. Nevada Fall usually comes to life later in the morning, when the light casts curious shadows on the cliff face.

To get there in the summer, take the shuttle to stop #16 at Happy Isles, where signs will guide you to the trailhead. In the winter, park in the day-use parking lot near Curry Village, and walk about fifteen minutes to Happy Isles, where the trail begins. To reach the bridge looking out onto Vernal Fall, you'll walk eight-tenths of a mile and gain 400 feet in elevation. To reach the falls' summits, there's a mile and a half hike with a thousand-foot gain to Vernal Fall, and a three and a half mile hike rising nineteen hundred feet to the top of Nevada Fall.

What kinds of animals live in the park?

We have 367 different kinds of wildlife, but the total animal population is actually quite small. This is due in part to our making room for animals of another kind: four million visitors a year.

Our spring and summer skies are filled with the colors and songs of 247 species of birds. Among our well-known year-round residents are the corn woodpecker, Steller's jay, and mountain chickadee.

Twelve species of fish swim our rivers and lakes, with just about every kind of trout, including cutthroat and rainbow. We also have a dozen types of frogs, toads, and salamanders, like the elusive Yosemite toad and limestone salamander. Hikers who are squeamish about snakes should make plenty of noise on the trail to scare away our sixteen kinds of reptiles, including the king snake and western rattlesnake.

Visitors will see more birds than mammals, even though we furry folk outnumber our feathered friends almost ten to one. Of our eighty different types of mammals, you're most likely to see squirrels and chipmunks picking up scraps around visitor areas. You might glimpse a deer, coyote, or one of us black bears, but you will probably only catch the tracks of a badger, bobcat, fox, or mountain lion.

The National Park Service protects the natural habitats of ten endangered or threatened species, including the bald eagle, peregrine falcon, and California wolverine. The rangers have also started a series of programs to restore natural wildlife habitats and protect visitors from injury and property damage. My favorite one is called "Don't Be Bear Careless."

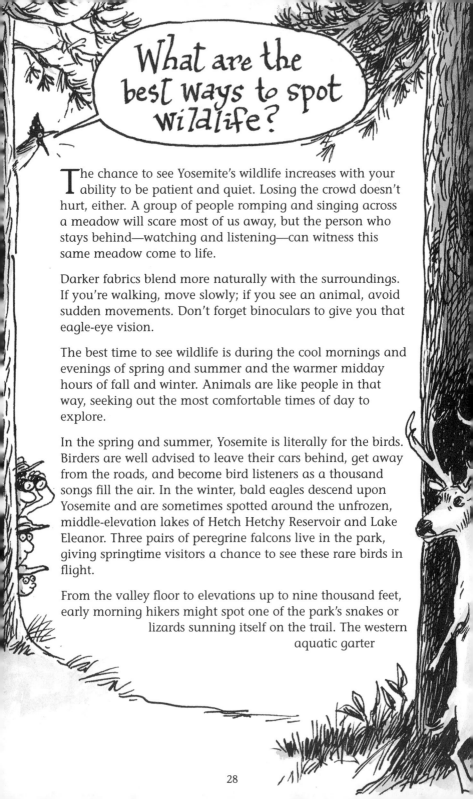

What are the best ways to spot wildlife?

The chance to see Yosemite's wildlife increases with your ability to be patient and quiet. Losing the crowd doesn't hurt, either. A group of people romping and singing across a meadow will scare most of us away, but the person who stays behind—watching and listening—can witness this same meadow come to life.

Darker fabrics blend more naturally with the surroundings. If you're walking, move slowly; if you see an animal, avoid sudden movements. Don't forget binoculars to give you that eagle-eye vision.

The best time to see wildlife is during the cool mornings and evenings of spring and summer and the warmer midday hours of fall and winter. Animals are like people in that way, seeking out the most comfortable times of day to explore.

In the spring and summer, Yosemite is literally for the birds. Birders are well advised to leave their cars behind, get away from the roads, and become bird listeners as a thousand songs fill the air. In the winter, bald eagles descend upon Yosemite and are sometimes spotted around the unfrozen, middle-elevation lakes of Hetch Hetchy Reservoir and Lake Eleanor. Three pairs of peregrine falcons live in the park, giving springtime visitors a chance to see these rare birds in flight.

From the valley floor to elevations up to nine thousand feet, early morning hikers might spot one of the park's snakes or lizards sunning itself on the trail. The western aquatic garter

snake is the exception, making its home in rivers and streams.

If you want to glimpse some of Yosemite's sixteen kinds of fish, approach the task with the care and timing of a master angler like me. Waiting on a lake's shore or stream's edge, you can watch them feeding, making circles in the still waters of early morning or late afternoon.

Chipmunks and squirrels are easy to find at most elevations. Just hang around a campground or picnic area and you'll see them gathering crumbs and other bits of trash, maybe even the food you still wanted. In the cool of the morning and early evening, mule deer are often seen grazing in small groups in the sunlit meadows and shadows of the oak groves. You might see coyote too, which hunt from the late afternoon on into the night.

Unlike me, most black bears are surprisingly shy but are sometimes seen foraging in the mountainous areas of the park in the early morning or late evening. Some of us have discovered that people leave behind food, so we might rummage around campgrounds late at night.

Don't try to get too close to the animals in the park. Feeding a chipmunk might seem like a fun idea, but all it takes is one sick animal to infect others, including humans. Deer shouldn't eat people-food either. A diet of old bread and cookies can harm their digestive systems and the milk they pass to their fawns. As for us bears, don't ever get between a cub and its protective mama.

Can we ever feed the animals?

Knock off the fatty foods.

Every time someone feeds an animal in the park, a little bit of the "wild" is stolen from our wildlife. Human food can not only damage the animals' health but also can change their behavior and endanger their survival by luring them away from their natural habits (and into the roads!).

Federal law prohibits people from feeding or approaching the park's wildlife, and for good reason. Our animals may look harmless, but any one of them is capable of causing infection, injury—and in extreme cases even death—to people who get too close. If an animal is aware of your presence, you're probably too close.

Remember, keeping food to yourself helps keep our wildlife wild and healthy.

YOSEMITE'S ENDANGERED OR THREATENED SPECIES

Endangered (Federal Government Lists)
Bald eagle
Peregrine falcon

Endangered (State of California Lists)
Bald eagle
Great gray owl
Peregrine falcon
Willow flycatcher

Threatened (State of California)
California bighorn sheep
California wolverine
Sierra Nevada red fox
Swainson's hawk

Rare Plant Species (State of California)
Congdon's lewisia
Congdon's woolly sunflower
Tompkin's sedge
Yosemite onion

Is it true bears are the most dangerous animals?

Even though I am the most powerful (not to mention the best-looking) animal in the park, I'm not the most dangerous to humans.

Does it surprise you to learn that the only death of a human by an animal in Yosemite's history was caused by a deer? Timid as they may seem, deer are wild animals, with sharp hoofs and antlers that can strike swiftly and without warning. Bucks are especially dangerous during spring's mating season.

Most injuries to people result from trying to get too close to animals—like when they try to feed the squirrels and raccoons by hand and end up getting scratched and bitten. Fleas carried by ground squirrels have been known to spread disease, even the bubonic plague. So don't be fooled into thinking the little cute ones are harmless.

With no wolves remaining, the coyote is the largest native dog in California. Yosemite's coyote are normally very shy, but they've become accustomed to all the visitors. Despite any resemblance they might have to your dog friends back home, they are wild and should be avoided.

With a natural fear of humans, mountain lions pose little threat to people in the park. These federally protected animals feed mostly on deer, a natural activity that helps keep our ecology in a delicate balance.

Because of our size and habits, Yosemite's black bears have a somewhat fearsome reputation. To be honest, some of it is deserved. Each year we cause more property damage than any other animal in the park. Let's just say it's best if people and bears maintain a "long-distance" relationship.

Any great birding spots?

Year-round, Yosemite Valley is where you'll find most of our bird species. They're all around you, in the dry woodlands, humid forests, thickets, shrubby hillsides, boggy meadows, and grass-covered slopes. Watch for our rare birds, like eagles and falcons, that normally winter in the valley.

On the way to the Arch Rock Entrance, a winter drive along Highway 140 in the Merced River canyon will take you by a great birding spot around El Portal. Wandering around the chaparral, oak woodlands, and slopes, you'll hear the songs of many of our common birds that favor the area's mild winters.

In the higher elevations, you should check out the bird life around Ackerson Meadow (forty-six hundred feet). This is the area along Ackerson Creek between the South and Middle Forks of the Tuolumne River. Although most of it is outside park boundaries, it's home to more than 150 species of birds from spring through fall.

During the spring and summer months, higher elevations like Tuolumne Meadows and along the Tioga Road are home to more than 140 bird species. If you're up for some high-altitude hiking, explore the bird habitats in the forests around Lembert and Pothole domes (nine thousand to ninety-four hundred feet) and the Hall Natural Area (ten to thirteen thousand feet).

If you forgot binoculars, you can rent a pair from Yosemite tour desks, lodgings, or retail shops.

Enough about animals! What kinds of flora will we see?

Yosemite is the land of evergreen. The various types of plants here outnumber our animal species three to one and come in as many shapes and sizes. Close your eyes in the meadow or forest; you'll hear the wind's voice in our more than fifteen hundred different plants and thirty-seven types of trees. From the giant sequoia that rise nearly three hundred feet in the air to ferns blanketing the forest floor, our world of flora is one of the park's greatest attractions.

Walk a few minutes from the Visitor Center and you'll pass through the sprawling shades of black and canyon oaks and see the tall ponderosa and a few lodgepole pines. Douglas firs and incense cedars flourish in the forests, with an occasional cottonwood, willow, alder, and azalea growing in moister areas.

Some of our pines have the sweet aroma of vanilla or pineapple, with long cones drooping like water drops from their upper branches. Our Pacific dogwood trees grow pale green flowers each spring, while the leaves of the quaking aspen turn golden in the fall.

The trails leading up out of the valley will bring you past sugar pines and white firs. Even higher, the flower-filled meadows and steep forest slopes are home to red firs and more sugar pines that reach two hundred feet in the air.

Walking along Tuolumne Meadows, you'll leave oaks and firs behind. At this elevation the meadows rule, bordered by lodgepole pines and a scattering of mountain hemlocks, quaking aspens, and Sierra junipers.

Was it something I said?

Where are the best places to see wildflowers?

Sprouting in the foothills in March, our wildflowers begin their six-month season. The valley blooms in May, and by August wildflowers spread their blanket of color to the park's high country.

As spring turns to summer, you can follow the blooms from Wawona Meadow in the south up to higher meadows like McGurk's and Mono. In the early spring, you'll find a great wildflower-covered trail starting at Savage's Trading Post in El Portal and leading up to the South Fork of the Merced. Around the same time, the violet family has moved into the valley. The Mountain Violet appears near Happy Isles and along the trail at Inspiration Point. The purple violet hangs out in the grass at the edge of Bridalveil Meadow, while the lone white violet keeps vigil in Leidig Meadow.

Summer brings azaleas to El Capitan Meadow and wild ginger along the trail from Mirror Lake to Snow Creek in Tenaya Canyon. Look for our pink to white pussy paws in the open, sunny flats of the valley, and the rose-and-silver tones of the showy milkweed in the valley's meadows.

By summer, the wildflowers have reached up into the rim country, where forests and meadows are crossed by streams and the two roads winding through wildflower havens. Take a

walk along the rim country's trails or drive Glacier Point and Tioga Roads to get an eyeful of early summer color, like the bright red of the mountain pride, the glowing pink of the shooting star, or the brilliant yellow of the California coneflower. If you're up to the adventure, try the Pohono Trail for a thirteen-mile, all-day hike through some our mid-elevation's most awesome wildflower scenery.

In August, the high country gets its own share of color. Driving east on the Tioga Road to the park's Tioga Pass Entrance, you'll find a wildflower bounty around Tuolumne Meadows, beaming with the magenta of the lemon bottlebrush, the soft yellow of buttercups, and the indigo hue of whorled penstemon.

When you've hiked as high as you can go, you won't see any more trees, but you'll still find wildflowers. Some of the high country trails, like in Dana Meadows, just east of Tioga Pass, and Long Meadow, near the Sunrise High Sierra Camp, take you past some awesome blooms.

To find out about some great wildflower books, refer to "Further Reading" on page 165, or visit one of the park's visitor centers.

In the fall, of course! In October and November, the rich colors of our trees and meadows are enough to make your eyes water, the leaves so heavy with red, gold, and green that they simply have to fall.

There are certain places in the park where you're sure to catch the season's best sights. In El Capitan Meadow, sprawling black oaks drop their red and golden leaves into the Merced River; on its banks the alder trees stand tall with yellow-green leaves set against their white bark. Other spots provide a sampling of just about every fall color, like Cook's Meadow, where the black oak, maple, and white alder paint the sky. Sometimes one tree, like the dogwood, often dresses in fall's coat of many colors.

Autumn is a great time to walk in the valley. Try the Mirror Lake trail with its honey-colored carpet of leaves that follows along Tenaya Creek. At midday, the sun shines through the trees' branches to the forest floor.

The trails of the south and north rim country will take you past pocket meadows and scatterings of trees drenched in autumn color. If you drive the Tioga, Glacier Point, or Wawona roads, you'll see vast meadows turned to fields of gold.

WOW!

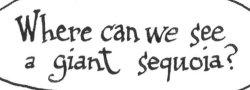

Where can we see a giant sequoia?

In the park there are three groves of giant sequoias, sometimes called Big Trees or Sierra redwoods. The largest of the three is the Mariposa Grove near Wawona at the southern border of the park. In the summer, trams take visitors on a tour of hundreds of trees, including the nearly three-thousand-year-old Grizzly Giant, with a branch that measures six feet around.

Tuolumne Grove is another good place for giant-hunting. Here lies the Dead Giant, which in its prime enjoyed celebrity status as the famous Mariposa Tunnel Tree (see next page). You can reach Tuolumne Grove by foot on a section of the old Big Oak Flat Road from Crane Flat.

Four miles south of the Tuolumne Grove is the Merced Grove, a little valley where wildflowers grow in spring and sequoias reach for the sky. Merced Grove is reached by foot along a two-mile dirt road off of Big Oak Flat Road.

Many visitors confuse the giant sequoias with their cousin, the coast redwoods, which have bragging rights for having the tallest tree in the world. Besides the difference in appearance (the sequoias' reddish gray bark compared to the deeper red color of the redwoods'), they grow in different regions. Redwoods are found between Northern California and Oregon along the fog-covered coast, while sequoias grow inland on the western slopes of the Sierra Nevada.

The redwoods may have the tallest single tree, but our sequoias' trunks have the largest measured diameters of any tree trunk in the world.

Redwood.   Sequoia!

What happened to the famous drive-through tree?

The story begins in 1878 with the tunneling of the first tree in Yosemite, a twenty-nine-and-a-half-foot-tall sequoia tree stump called the "Dead Giant" in the Tuolumne Grove. Then, in 1881 a man named Albert Henry Washburn came along. As head of the Yosemite Stage and Turnpike Company and owner of the newly built Wawona Hotel, Washburn had a keen interest in tourist traffic. He set out to build a new road so visitors could travel with ease from the lower to the upper sequoia groves.

There was one thing standing in his way: a two-thousand-year-old, 234-foot tall giant sequoia.

Washburn, known as "the transportation king of the Sierra," would not be stopped. His team cut an eight-foot-wide, ten-foot-high, and twenty-six-foot-long hole through the tree—big enough for a horse and wagon to roll through. The Mariposa Tunnel Tree quickly became a major park attraction, drawing visitors from around the world. But it was not to last.

With a hole in the heart of its trunk and the adverse effects of a severe snowstorm, the sequoia fell in the winter of 1968–1969.

Park visitors then turned more attention to the Dead Giant in the Tuolumne Grove, flocking to this tunnel tree until the summer of 1993, when park officials closed off car traffic due to damage to the grove's ecosystem. Today, only those on foot can go through the Dead Giant, and they can get there by taking the old Big Oak Flat Road from Crane Flat to Tuolumne Grove.

EXCUSE ME !! WHERE CAN WE DRIVE INTO A TREE?

PARK RANGER

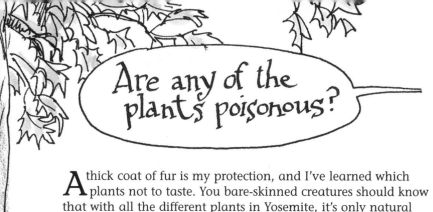

Are any of the plants poisonous?

A thick coat of fur is my protection, and I've learned which plants not to taste. You bare-skinned creatures should know that with all the different plants in Yosemite, it's only natural that some have a bit of a nasty side to them. Not to worry, though: any threat from these plants-with-attitudes is generally not serious and can easily be avoided with a little caution.

Poison oak dwells in the shady areas of the park's lower elevations. It's quite the chameleon, changing from green in spring to red in autumn, but it's almost always identifiable by its three leaves. The oil from this sneaky plant can cause a rash a few days after contact, at which time your skin will swell and itch. If you think you might have touched poison oak, wash your body with cold water to close your pores and get rid of the oils.

Walking through the meadows in the valley, you might also feel the prickly sting of nettles. They hide in the meadow grasses, so keep a sharp eye out for where you're stepping in the fields. Rangers ask that you stick to established trails, to protect both the plants and yourselves!

Coming across wild mushrooms isn't dangerous, as long as you look instead of touch. Whatever you do, never eat a mushroom from the wild. If you touch one, like the deadly Amanitus, make sure you wash your hands thoroughly.

Pants and long sleeves will help if you decide to venture off-trail, or you can just stay clear of plant trouble altogether by sticking to the well-worn paths.

It's a jungle out there.

What was life like for Yosemite's native peoples?

Imagine Yosemite long before it was a national park: no cars or roads, no buildings or parking lots, but water still plunging in great falls and wildflowers still blanketing the valley's meadows in spring. People were living here four thousand years before the Spanish arrived and gold was discovered in the hills, and they called their home Ahwahnee ("place of a gaping mouth") and themselves, the Ahwahneechee. Today, we know them as the Yosemite Miwoks.

Until gold miners arrived in the mid 1800s, the Miwok people lived a relatively unchanged lifestyle in Yosemite. They gathered seeds and plants, hunted game, and traded with other tribes from the east. The Miwoks practiced very little cultivation, moving from the higher elevations in spring and summer to the warmer foothills and valley in fall and winter. This lifestyle proved to be very gentle on the land. Today, the traces of their existence are found in artifacts like obsidian tools and granite grinding rocks.

They built cedar bark homes and earth-covered gathering halls. Acorns provided a food staple, prepared and eaten as mush and combined with veggies like mushrooms, ferns, clover, and bulbs. With bows and arrows they hunted deer, rabbits, and squirrels and fished the rivers and streams for trout and Sacramento suckers. Some insects like fly larvae, caterpillars, and grasshoppers were delicacies.

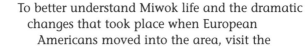

BEAR RIGHT.

To better understand Miwok life and the dramatic changes that took place when European Americans moved into the area, visit the re-created Indian village and cultural exhibit near the Valley Visitor Center.

When did the first Euro-American pioneers come to Yosemite?

In 1851, a group of men formed a small army called the Mariposa Battalion to attack the Yosemite Miwok, who had defended their homeland against gold miners settling in the area. The battalion drove the Miwoks from Yosemite, and forever changed the land once known as Ahwahnee.

A San Franciscan (originally from England) named James Mason Hutchings read about the Mariposa Battalion in the newspaper and decided to see the place for himself. Inspired by the sight of Yosemite, Hutchings organized the first tourist party to the valley in 1855. The word was out.

Tourists, homesteaders, and folks with money on their mind flocked to the area—first on foot and horseback, then by wagon and stage-coach—and soon there were hotels, roads, homes, livestock, orchards, crops, and stores in the valley. By the late 1860s the valley was bustling with private businesses cashing in on Yosemite's new-found popularity.

Overuse of the land worried some people. Early conservationists like I. W. Raymond and Frederick Law Olmstead, both with friends in high places, asked the government for help. By 1864, they got a bill passed by Congress and signed by President Abraham Lincoln giving Yosemite Valley and the Mariposa Grove of Big Trees to the state of California to preserve and protect. Yosemite became the world's first government-protected natural area, marking the beginning of the state and national park systems in the United States.

I preferred things the way they were before the last ice age.

To learn more about the pioneer days in Yosemite, visit the Pioneer Yosemite History Center in Wawona, or check out some of the books listed in "Further Reading" on page 165.

PIONEER YOSEMITE HISTORY CENTER

What role did the U.S. Army play in the history of Yosemite?

As far as army posts go, they don't get much better than this. Soon after Congress declared Yosemite a national park on October 1, 1890, Captain A. E. Woods and his U.S. Army troops arrived in Yosemite to act as the original park caretakers and administrators. In 1914, the troops handed the reins over to the first civilian National Park Service staff, but not before paving the way for today's Yosemite.

In the spring of 1891, the army set up Camp A. E. Woods just north of Wawona, along with many small patrol camps around the park. Their first battle was against the sheepherders, whose livestock was chowing down on Yosemite's high country. Next came the dirty work of preparing a national park.

They covered every inch of the park, mapping and marking its boundaries, blazing trails and building bridges, stocking lakes and rivers, fighting fires, and confiscating guns from unruly visitors and residents.

By 1906, it was time to further civilize the valley. Captain Harry C. Benson and his 6th Cavalry established Fort Yosemite on the site where the Yosemite Lodge sits today and quickly got down to the business of building sanitation facilities to stop raw sewage from polluting streams and rivers. They also rid the valley of firearms and animal traps laid by settlers, and in 1912 they built the Yosemite Hospital. The next year, the first automobiles started rolling into the valley, so the troops enforced the speed limits of fifteen miles per hour in the valley and five miles per hour on steep descents.

The Army left behind their bridges, their trails, their maps...

...And their hats!

42

Didn't Ansel Adams take a lot of pictures of Half Dome?

I don't recall his taking pictures of any bears, but Ansel Adams did take many famous photographs of Yosemite, including ones of Half Dome. He first set foot in the park in 1916, armed with a new gift: a box camera. By the late 1920s Adams was working for the Yosemite Park & Curry Company, which hired him to take pictures of the park for newspapers and magazines. It was the beginning of a life-long love for Yosemite and also the start of his efforts as a leading conservationist in California.

Adams's photographs became famous worldwide. Even after his death in 1984, his pictures live on, and many visitors still flock to the park just to see the images that he captured through his lens.

Today, Adams's original artwork can be admired and pur-chased at the Ansel Adams Gallery next to the Visitor Center in Yosemite Village. The gallery also rents cameras and leads camera walks so you can search for your own Yosemite mas-terpiece. For more information, call (209) 372-4413.

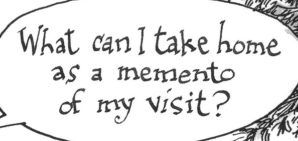

What can I take home as a memento of my visit?

With an awe-inspiring backdrop like Yosemite, anyone with a camera can take home some of the magic without stealing anything away from the beauty of the park. There are no mementos quite like the photographs which capture and give life to special memories, such as that of a snowshoed walk through Tuolumne Meadows or a hike up Mist Trail.

For less adventuresome keepsakes, check out the park shops, galleries, and museums. Besides the ever-popular T-shirts and mugs, there are a wide range of gifts that evoke the spirit of Yosemite, including jewelry carved with the images of local flora and fauna, candles with pressed wildflowers, Indian arrowheads and crafts, and everything Ansel Adams, from postcards to original prints selling for thousands of dollars.

The search for souvenirs can become a problem in our park. That's why people are prohibited from destroying or removing just about everything in the park, including plants, animals, minerals, and archeological artifacts. A family driving out with a basketful of pine cones shouldn't be surprised if the ranger hands over a $50 to $100 citation—one of the less desirable of Yosemite mementos.

These regulations are designed to keep Yosemite intact despite the four million visitors a year who want to take a piece of it home. Just think, if everyone started chipping away a piece of Half Dome, it would soon become Quarter Dome.

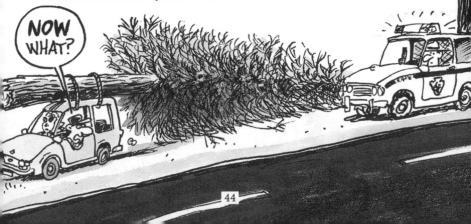

NOW WHAT?

What's the best way to see the park?

Free Shuttles

I'll bet John Muir never would have guessed there'd one day be a shuttle in Yosemite Valley taking people wherever they wanted to go. We haven't figured out how to get one up Half Dome yet, but we do have a shuttle that takes visitors to nineteen other most popular spots in Yosemite Valley. This is the only year-round free shuttle, and it operates from 7 a.m. to 10 p.m. spring through fall and from 9 a.m. to 10 p.m. in the winter, arriving at each stop every few minutes during the busy summer and every twenty minutes in the winter. Remember, you're just one of twenty-five thousand shuttle riders in the peak season, so be ready to wait in line. (See map on page 49.)

In Wawona, a free shuttle runs to the South Entrance station and on to the Mariposa Grove and Wawona Grocery Store from 9 a.m. to 6 p.m., spring through the first week of October. In the summer and early fall, shuttles are available in Tuolumne Meadows during daylight hours, taking visitors from the Tuolumne Lodge to the west end of Tenaya Lake, with several stops in between. Skiers can ride a winter shuttle to and from the Badger Pass slopes, with three other stops on the route. For more shuttle information call (209) 372-1240.

Tram Tours

A two-hour narrated park tour in an open-air tram (weather permitting) costs $16 for adults and $8.50 for children ages five to twelve, and operates year-round from 9 a.m. to 5 p.m., spring to fall, and 9 a.m. to 3 p.m. in the winter. The tour starts at Yosemite Lodge, in Curry Village, the Ahwahnee hotel, and in the summer at the tour kiosk behind the Village Store. Between 9 a.m. and 5:30 p.m. in the summer, Wawona has a daily, one-hour tram tour through the Mariposa Grove of Big Trees. It boards at Mariposa Grove every twenty minutes; cost is $8 for adults, $7.25 for seniors, and $4 for children ages four to twelve, with a $24 maximum per family.

Bus Tours

From spring through Labor Day, buses run from Yosemite Lodge to Glacier Point (4 hours/$20 round trip), Mariposa Grove (6 hours/$34), Tuolumne Meadows (the Hikers' Bus costs $20 round trip), and around the valley by moonlight ($16). Reservations can be made at the tour kiosks at Yosemite Village and Curry Village spring through fall, or by calling (209) 372-1240 year-round.

Autos

Determined drivers can visit quite a few park areas, many with turnouts and informational signs. You can buy a two- to four-hour audio tour of the park at the Valley Visitor Center. Remember, Yosemite Valley and the Mariposa Grove always have tons of traffic, and cars are not allowed on the Happy Isles Loop, Mirror Lake/Meadow roads, or the roads through Yosemite Village. For road conditions, call (209) 372-0200.

Bikes

With over eight miles of well-marked bike paths, bicycling is a fun and safe way to get around the park; just stay on the paved paths and roads, and wear a helmet. You can rent bikes and helmets by the hour ($5.25) or for the day ($20) at the Yosemite Lodge or Curry Village every day, conditions permitting (see page 108 in the Recreational Opportunities section for more information on biking).

Walking

The best way to escape the crowds and see Yosemite's finer points is to hoof it, hiking or backpacking through some of the eight hundred miles of developed trails within park boundaries. These hikes range from easy walks along the valley floor to steeper treks to Upper Yosemite Falls, Mirror Lake, and Vernal Fall. You should know your limits before embarking on one of these journeys, and remember to bring water. Take a look at pages 98–107 in the Recreational Opportunities section to find out about some great day hikes. You might also want to stop at the Wilderness Center next to the post office in Yosemite Village.

Others

Cross-country skiing is a great way to traverse the park during the snowy months. In the summer, you can let a horse do all the work on two-hour, four-hour, or all-day rides that start from the stables in Wawona and Tuolumne Meadows. There are no longer any stables in Yosemite Valley. Children must be age seven or older to ride. For telephone numbers, see our telephone directory that starts on page 151.

Where are the Yosemite Valley shuttle bus stops?

Almost anywhere you find yourself in the eastern end of the valley there's a shuttle bus stop nearby. From spring through fall the buses run every ten minutes or so between 7 a.m. and 10 p.m. In the winter, the buses run a little less often between the hours of 9 a.m. and 10 p.m. There are stops that access the major campgrounds, Yosemite Lodge, Camp Curry and the Ahwahnee Hotel, Yosemite Village with all its services and shops, and some of the more scenic trails in the valley. The buses even take you to areas such as Happy Isles and Mirror Lake, which are closed to private automobiles. In winter, shuttle service is discontinued to Happy Isles, Mirror Lake/Meadow, and the Stables.

HERE'S A LIST OF THE SHUTTLE STOPS:

1   Day Use Parking/Curry Village
2   Upper and Lower River Campgrounds
          (destroyed by flood in 1997)
3   Yosemite Village/Visitor Center
4   The Ahwahnee Hotel
5   Yosemite Village
6   Visitor Center
7   Yosemite Falls (service until 8 p.m.)
8   Yosemite Lodge/Sunnyside Walk-In Campground
9   Visitor Center
10   Yosemite Village
11   Sentinel Bridge/Parking for Yosemite Chapel
12   Housekeeping Camp/LeConte Memorial
13   Ice Rink (winter only)
14   Day-Use Parking/Curry Village
15   Upper Pines Campground
16   Happy Isles (service until 7:30 p.m.)
17   Mirror Lake/Meadow (service until 7:30 p.m.)
18   Stables (service until 7:30 p.m.)
19   Lower Pines Campground

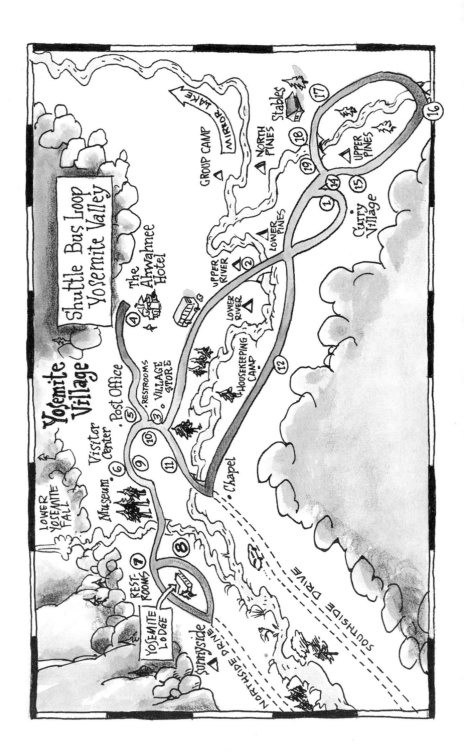

Where are the best spots and what are the best times to take pictures in Yosemite Valley?

Whether an autumn leaf or the heights of Half Dome, a great subject for a memorable Yosemite snapshot is around every turn. The light will bring these pictures to life, and every hour of the day offers different shading.

Yosemite and Nevada Falls go through many changes in the course of a day. At mid-morning, the sun casts shadows and light on the falling water. Later in the afternoon, the falls cast their own shadows on the cliff and stand out clearly from the rock face.

Spring is the best season to capture our waterfalls. At Bridalveil Fall, the shadows lift at midday to reveal a sunlit mist at its top that helps people understand its name.

A stroll between 10 a.m. and noon from the Happy Isles Nature Center to Vernal Fall reaps photo riches, with the light changing the water into falling jewels.

During spring, Mirror Lake lives up to its name until about 8 a.m., when the sun steals its reflection. Don't be discouraged if the day is overcast; on a cloudy day the lake's mirror is often at its clearest, and the light has a nice even tone by which to take shots of the lake's scenic views of Half Dome.

The fun part is finding your own perfect scene to capture on film. From El Capitan to a secret trail, your memories of the park's beauty are only a click away. For more information on free guided photo walks, call the tour desk at Yosemite Lodge (209/372-1240).

One of the best places in the Valley to take pictures is behind the camera!

Are there any self-guided tours?

You'll find plenty of ways to lead your own tours in the park. You can start in the Yosemite Museum, where you'll learn about Yosemite's human and natural history, then take the one-mile "Changing Yosemite" nature walk trail.

History buffs can visit the museum's American Indian cultural exhibit, then take a short, self-guided walk through a re-created Miwok Indian village. The Pioneer Yosemite History Center in Wawona offers a thirty-minute, self-guided tour that reveals the lifestyles of Yosemite's early pioneers.

Self-guided tours also let you venture into the wild. Yosemite has a number of walking trails with signs along the way, teaching visitors about plant life, native animals, history, and special geographic features. Giant sequoia seekers can take a half-mile, self-guided tour of Tuolumne Grove or the slightly longer walk through Mariposa Grove, which leads to the famous Grizzly Giant. Starting at the Glen Aulin trailhead in Tuolumne Meadows, there's a one-mile trail to Soda Springs that takes you to the spot where John Muir and Robert Johnson thought up the idea of a National Park.

Do-it-yourself road adventures are found in the pages of the *Yosemite Road Guide* ($3.50), which steers you to more than 120 roadside markers, each offering interesting bits of information about Yosemite's natural features and history. Or you can buy a two-hour audio tour for $9.95 and see ten valley sites by car. Both the guide and the audio tour can be purchased at the Valley Visitor Center.

Um... tree!

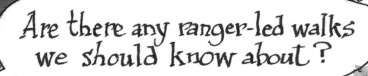

The best way to unlock the mysteries of Yosemite is to hang out with the people that have the keys: the Yosemite rangers, the ones wearing Smokey-the-Bear hats.

In the valley, rangers lead a series of free ninety-minute to two-hour narrated walks on various subjects, including wildlife, geography, and park history. Most of these informative tours start from Happy Isles or the Valley Visitor Center. The kids can get their own special tours from the Sierra Club's sixty- to ninety-minute nature walks, starting from the LeConte Memorial (shuttle stop #12). Guides are also on hand to lead visitors on a few unique walks, like the one that focuses on the history of climbing in Yosemite and another that features the best places to take pictures. There is even a stroll led by a guide who looks and acts just like John Muir. For times and seasonal schedules, call the park's information line at (209) 372-0265, or check the *Yosemite Guide*.

Mariposa Grove rangers lead visitors on ninety-minute and three-hour walks through the grove in the summer, explaining the many wonders of the sequoia forests. Walks start from the trailhead parking lot several times each day. The Wawona Information Station offers similar tours of the area, led by naturalists and park historians. Check the bulletin board at the Mariposa Grove trailhead, or call the Wawona Information Station at (209) 375-9501.

Does anyone in the group have any idea how old this giant sequoia is?

Tuolumne Grove has its own share of giant sequoias that you can explore on a two-and-a-half-hour, ranger-led walk departing from the Tuolumne Grove parking area. For schedule information, call the Big Oak Flat Information Station at (209) 379-1899.

The magical red fir forests and awesome views at Glacier Point become even more amazing on two-hour ranger walks, meeting at the Taft Point/Sentinel Dome parking area, Mondays and Tuesdays, at 2 p.m. (from spring through October). You can also explore Yosemite's sky on a thirty-minute sunset tour and one-hour "Stars Over Yosemite" walk. In Tuolumne Meadows, rangers lead morning, noon, and afternoon nature walks ranging from one to four miles in length. You can picnic with your guide while you learn about the natural and human history of Yosemite's subalpine areas. For information on all of these walks, call the Tuolumne Meadows Visitor Center at (209) 372-0263 (summer only).

Rangers lead snowshoe walks every day that the Badger Pass ski area is fully operational in the winter. For information, call (209) 372-0265.

Are there any guided trips into Yosemite's high country?

A journey into Yosemite's high country isn't exactly a walk in the valley. You need to be in good shape to tackle these trails and should plan on spending a day prior to your trip acclimating to the higher elevations.

For those ready to take on a week-long hike, there's a guided tour covering from five to ten miles each day, stopping at five High Sierra Camps, and climbing just over ten thousand feet. Experienced rangers lead these high country excursions, offering hikers a deeper understanding of Yosemite and its natural and human histories. This adventure embarks twice a week from the Tuolumne Meadows Lodge between June and early September. The cost is approximately $735 per person for six nights lodging and all meals. For more information, call the High Sierra desk at (209) 253-5674.

You can also experience high country excitement sitting atop a saddle. Scenic horseback trips, led by knowledgeable guides, depart daily on two-hour, half-day, and all-day rides from Wawona and Tuolumne Meadows from June to Labor Day. If you don't get too saddle-sore, you can try a six-day (around $870 per person) or four-day (around $550 per person) saddle tour into the high country. Prices include lodging and all meals at the High Sierra Camps. For more information and reservations, call (209) 372-8384.

In winter, you can glide your way across the high country slopes by taking a cross-country ski tour with the Badger Pass ski school. For more details, call (209) 372-8444.

Whew!

How does winter change getting around in the park?

Winter's big freeze closes off Tioga Road and Glacier Point Road (from Badger Pass ski area). With the help of a snowplow, the rest of the park stays open all winter, unless there's a monster snowfall that makes it impossible to clear the roads.

Highway 140, going through Merced, Mariposa, and the Arch Rock Entrance, seems to get the least of winter's fury. Highways 120 and 41 from the west often get a heavy dose of snow, requiring drivers to practice their skills at putting on tire chains. But once you're in the valley, you can usually rely on the snowplows doing their job.

We try to keep the Tioga and Glacier Point Roads open until November 1, but we've had some nasty snowstorms close these routes as early as September. Rockslides, fires, and other problems pop up every now and then to cause closures, as well.

Winter driving in Yosemite can be dangerous. With the roads covered with snow and hard-to-see ice, you'll need to slow down and carry a set of chains at all times. Keep a sharp eye out for snowplows, and use those turnouts if you need to stop for a while. For twenty-four-hour road conditions in Yosemite, call (209) 372-0200 (recording), or (209) 372-0265 Monday through Friday, 9–12 and 1–5.

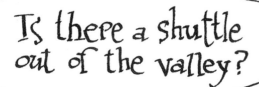

From July 4 through the Sunday following Labor Day, we have a special shuttle called the Hikers' Bus, which takes visitors from the valley to Tuolumne Meadows and to all the Tioga Road trailheads in between. Buses depart each morning from Curry Village, Yosemite Village, the Ahwahnee hotel, and Yosemite Lodge for this all-day scenic tour, at a cost of $20 round-trip or $13 one-way. Along with all the major trailheads, the Hikers' Bus stops at Crane Flat and White Wolf and the scenic spots at Olmstead Point and Tenaya Lake lookout. Call (209) 372-8441 for information and reservations.

The Yosemite Valley-to-Glacier Point route also has a hikers' bus of its own from late spring to early fall. With a one-way ticket selling for $10.50, hikers can ride the bus to Glacier Point and walk down to the valley along the four-mile or Panorama Trail, or hike up to Glacier Point and catch a ride back down to the valley. Another option is just taking a four-hour round-trip tour for $20.00 (prices subject to change).

Tickets are available at all hotel tour desks and the Village Store tour kiosk. Call (209) 372-1240 for reservations and schedule changes, or check the *Yosemite Guide*.

HIKERS' BUS SHUTTLE

Phone: (209) 372-8441

$13.00 one-way to Tuolumne Meadows, $20.00 same-day, round-trip
Schedule: (July 4 through the Sunday following Labor Day, conditions permitting)

Curry Village to Tuolumne Lodge (Read DOWN)		Tuolumne Lodge to Curry Village (Read UP)
Lv 8:20 a.m.	Curry Village	Ar 4:30 p.m.
Lv 8:25 a.m.	Yosemite Village	Ar 4:35 p.m.
Lv 8:45 a.m.	Yosemite Lodge	Ar 4:45 p.m.
Ar 9:15 a.m.	Crane Flat	Lv 3:40 p.m.
Lv 9:30 a.m.	Crane Flat	No time given
Lv 9:50 a.m.	White Wolf	Lv 3:35 p.m.
Lv 10:10 a.m.	May Lake Junction	Lv 3:00 p.m.
Lv 10:25 a.m.	Olmstead Point	No time given
Lv 10:30 a.m.	Tenaya Lake	Lv 3:00 p.m.
Ar 10:45 a.m.	Tuolumne Store	Lv 2:45 p.m.
Ar 10:55 a.m.	Tuolumne Lodge	Lv 2:35 p.m.

Employees and children ages 5 to 12 years old are charged half-price.
Children four years old and younger ride free of charge.
Bus can be flagged for pick-up at any trailhead, and passengers may request any trailhead for drop-off.

GLACIER POINT HALF-DAY TOUR & HIKERS' SHUTTLE

Phone: (209) 372-1240

Cost:	Adults	$20.00 round trip
	Children (5–12 years)	$10.50 round trip
	One-way	$10.50
	One-way child	$5.00

Last bus leaves Glacier Point at 3:00 p.m.

Operates daily while the Glacier Point Road is open

Curry Village	Yosemite Village	Ahwahnee Hotel	Yosemite Lodge
8:00 a.m.	8:05 a.m.	8:15 a.m.	8:30 a.m.
9:30 a.m.	9:35 a.m.	9:45 a.m.	10:00 a.m.
1:00 p.m.	1:95 p.m.	1:15 p.m.	1:30 p.m.

Hikers wishing to walk up to Glacier Point and catch the bus back may not reserve space on the bus and should be aware that seating availability is questionable for the return trip.

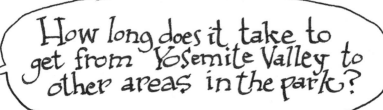

For most visitors, the valley is the perfect springboard for other park excursions. To get to other areas, follow the "All Park Exits" signs leading to a one-way road out of the valley. From here, you'll see exit signs for Highway 41 to Fresno, 140 to Merced, 120 to Manteca, and 120 east to the Tioga Road.

Heading south on Highway 41, you travel about an hour to get to Glacier Point (closed in winter) or Wawona and the Pioneer Yosemite History Center. A short drive south from Wawona, you'll arrive at the Mariposa Grove of Big Trees, where you can park and take the shuttle or walk into the grove. (In the summer you should plan to park your car in Wawona and take the free shuttle to the Mariposa Grove.)

Taking Highway 120 westward, you'll reach Crane Flat in about thirty minutes. A bit further and you'll arrive at the Tuolumne and Merced Groves of Big Trees. It's a steep, two-mile, round-trip hike to Tuolumne Grove and a two-and-a-half-mile walk to Merced Grove. Near the Big Oak Flat Entrance, you can turn right toward Hetch Hetchy (no vehicles over twenty-five feet in length), an hour-and-a-half drive from the valley.

The Tioga Road to the east (closed in winter) passes White Wolf, Tenaya Lake, and, after an hour and a half, Tuolumne Meadows. Fifteen minutes more and you'll cross the highest paved pass in the Sierra: the nearly ten-thousand-foot Tioga Pass.

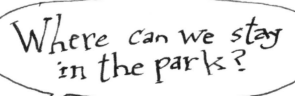

Where can we stay in the park?

After a long day roaming around Yosemite, a hot shower and a comfortable bed can do wonders for you. Luckily, you have close to fifteen hundred overnight accommodations in the park to choose from. Reservations for most lodgings are made through the Yosemite Concessions Services by phone (209/252-4848), or by sending a reservation request form (see pages 148 and 149) to Yosemite Reservations, 5410 E. Home, Fresno, CA 93727.

YOSEMITE VALLEY

If you're willing to pay for comfort, the **Ahwahnee hotel** can be mighty tempting. This National Historic Landmark is the lap of luxury, with 123 rooms, views of Glacier Point and the valley's south wall, private cottages, and prices ranging from $229 for a standard room to $750 for a three-room suite. It's truly fit for a queen, as the Queen of England decided when she stayed in the penthouse in 1983. There are slightly reduced rates Sunday through Thursday in the winter months.

One of the 249 rooms in the **Yosemite Lodge** is a good choice after your excursions to nearby attractions like Yosemite Falls and the Merced River. Prices range from $117 for deluxe rooms with balconies to $100 for standard rooms with baths. The lodge with pool and many services is open year-round.

For more modest digs and prices, **Curry Village** has rooms with baths for around $80, cabins with private ($82) and shared ($65) baths, and canvas tent cabins with communal baths ($46). It's open year-round and is close to Glacier Point and Happy Isles.

Housekeeping Camp is a camping experience with a few basic amenities. For about $43 you get a campsite with covered shelter, cots, and a table, while you provide the linens, sleeping bags, and cooking stuff. Located next to the Merced River, Housekeeping Camp also offers public showers, a store, and a laundromat, and it is open summers only.

SOUTH YOSEMITE

The **Wawona Hotel** is another National Historic Landmark; it's also the oldest resort hotel in California. The Wawona offers old-fashioned luxury: Victorian buildings, 100 rooms and cottages, wide porches looking out on green lawns, a swimming pool, tennis courts, and a nine-hole golf course. The rooms with private baths cost $113, and those that share a community bathroom cost $80. It's open from Easter week through October, plus weekends and holidays through Christmas. Call (209) 375-6556 for reservations.

The **Redwood Guest Cottages** are privately owned vacation homes available by the day or week, all with kitchens and fireplaces. Costs range from $82 to $365 per night, year-round. Call (209) 375-6666. Eight miles from Badger Pass and a thirty-minute drive from the valley, **Yosemite West Cottages** have units with TV, kitchens, and range ovens from $85 to $225 per night, year-round. Call (209) 642-2211.

NORTH YOSEMITE

The park's northern region offers accommodations in the summer only. On the road to Hetch Hetchy, the **Evergreen Lodge** has twenty-one rustic cabins (with baths) sleeping two people ($70) or up to four people ($80–$105), with continental breakfast included. There are no kitchens, but a restaurant, bar, and small store are nearby. Call (209) 379-2606. **White Wolf Lodge** also has rustic cabins with private baths ($50), tent cabins ($30) with shared bath and shower facilities, and a dining room and store. Near the Tuolumne River, the **Tuolumne Meadows Lodge** has sixty-nine canvas tent cabins ($30) with four beds, a wood stove, and candles (no electricity). Bathrooms and showers are communal. This place is popular, so reserve early. You can book rooms at both of these lodges by calling (209) 252-4848.

THE AHWAHNEE HOTEL

Celebrities who have stayed at the Ahwahnee hotel:
>   Ansel Adams, frequently between 1927 and his death in 1984
>   President Herbert Hoover in 1927, 1953, and 1960
>   President Franklin D. Roosevelt in 1938
>   Walt Disney in 1941
>   King Baudoin of Belgium in 1959
>   President John F. Kennedy in 1962
>   Queen Elizabeth II of England and Prince Philip in 1983
>   Actor Mel Gibson in 1992, during the filming of Maverick
>   Actor Robert Redford, a frequent visitor to the hotel
>   Sir Edmund Hillary, 1995 and 1996

Funny Celebrity Stories:
- Ahwahnee guests complained one evening about the loud music coming from the hotel lounge. The manager reluctantly asked Lucille Ball and Judy Garland to stop singing and playing the piano.
- When former president Herbert Hoover returned one afternoon from a day of fishing, a new Ahwahnee doorman politely turned him away due to Hoover's inappropriate attire.

Other National Park projects designed by the Ahwahnee hotel architect, Gilbert Stanley Underwood:
>   The Lodge at Zion National Park
>   Canyon Lodge at Bryce Canyon National Park
>   North Rim Lodge at Grand Canyon National Park

Are there any convenient places to stay outside Yosemite?

No matter what direction you're coming from, there are lots of places to stay just outside the park's four entrances.

HIGHWAY 41 FROM FRESNO

50 miles from the south entrance, in Oakhurst:

Oakhurst Lodge — 60 units
(209) 683-4417 — $57 all year

Shilo Inn — 80 units/pool
(209) 683-3555 — $69–$135/winter, $88–$135/summer

Yosemite Gateway Best Western — 118 units/2 pools and spas
(209) 683-2378 — $44–$80/winter, $78–$124/summer

Holiday Inn Express — 42 units/pool
(209) 642-2525 — $49–$69/winter, $69–$149/summer

37 miles from the south entrance, in Fish Camp

Marriott's Tenaya Lodge — 242 units/2 pools and fitness center
(209) 683-6555 — $89–$159/winter, $159–$239/summer

Narrow Gauge Inn — 27 units/pool
(209) 683-7720 — Closed in winter, $85–$120/summer

HIGHWAY 120 (EAST) FROM LEE VINING

74 miles from the Tioga Pass entrance, in Lee Vining:

Best Western Lakeview Lodge — 47 units
(619) 647-6543/(800) 528-1234 — $53–$150 all year

Tioga Pass Resort — 10 housekeeping cabins
(209) 372-4471 — weekly rentals only (Saturday–Saturday)
$430–$550/week
4 motel units: $50–$60 all year

HIGHWAY 140 FROM MERCED

43 miles from the Arch Rock Entrance, in Mariposa:

Holiday Inn Express   46 units
(209) 966-4288 $39–$69/winter, $79–$129/summer

Mariposa Lodge   37 units/pool, pets allowed
(209) 966-3607 $35–$65/winter, $65–$99/summer

Mother Lode Lodge   12 units/one kitchenette, pool
(209) 966-2521 $39–$55 all year

14 miles from the Arch Rock Entrance, in El Portal

Cedar Lodge   122 units/pool
(209) 379-2612 $80–$395 all year

Yosemite Redbud Lodge   8 units/some kitchenettes
(209) 379-2301 $75–$115 all year

Yosemite View Lodge   91 units/pool
(209) 379-2681/(800) 321-5261 $55–$139 all year

HIGHWAY 120 FROM MANTECA

37 miles from the Big Oak Flat Entrance, in Buck Meadows:

Buck Meadows Lodge   11 units
(209) 962-4922 $39–$69 all year

Yosemite Westgate Motel   45 units
(209) 962-5281 $49–$99 all year

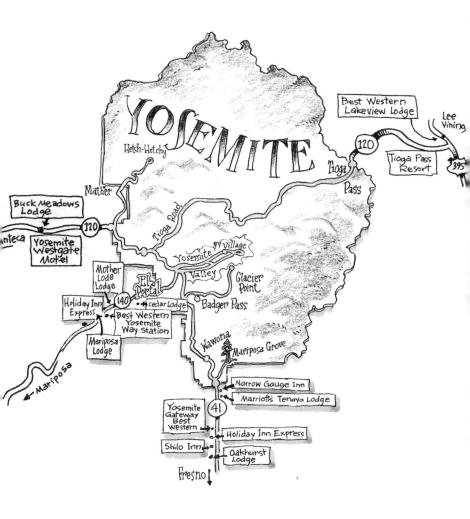

Where can we eat in the park?

YOSEMITE VALLEY
Yosemite Lodge
The Lodge's **Cafeteria** offers inexpensive meals year-round for breakfast, lunch, dinner. The **Garden Terrace** restaurant, open summers for breakfast, lunch, and dinner, offers an all-you-can-eat buffet with inexpensive to moderate prices. Reservations aren't accepted, and on weekends and holidays you can expect a wait. For a full-service restaurant with newly remodeled digs and great views, try the **Mountain Room**, open spring to fall, with outdoor dining in the summer. It has moderate-to-expensive prices, and the same no-reservations system as the Garden Terrace. The Lodge also offers poolside refreshments in summer.

Yosemite Village
Try **Degnan's Deli** for sandwiches and salads, or **Degnan's Fast Food** for stuff like pizza, chicken, frozen yogurt, and ice cream. Both are inexpensive and open year-round. From spring to fall, **The Pasta Place** offers moderately priced lunches and dinners, while the **Village Grill** serves inexpensive breakfasts, lunches, and dinners at an outside seating area.

Curry Village
The **Cafeteria** has a real mountain feel, with a chuckwagon barbeque line in the summer, a rustic atmosphere, and inexpensive prices. **The Hamburger Deck** serves your basic fare all day, spring to fall, and the **Pizza Deck**—you guessed it—serves pizza on a deck from spring to fall.

The Ahwahnee
Almost as great as Yosemite's natural treasures is a meal in the **Ahwahnee Dining Room**. Breakfast and lunch are casual dress, but coats and ties are preferred at dinner. Moderate to expensive. Dinner reservations are a must. Call (209) 372-1489. **The Ahwahnee Indian Room** lounge offers a limited menu, the same one you'll find poolside.

SOUTH YOSEMITE

The Wawona Hotel Dining Room provides the area's only full-service fine dining. Lunch and Sunday brunch are served buffet style, and in the summer you can try the Saturday barbecue on the hotel lawn (moderate to expensive). Reservations are not accepted. At the Wawona **Golf Shop Snack Bar**, you can watch the golfers while you munch on hot dogs, sandwiches, and other simple fare. Open summer and fall, the **Glacier Point Snack Stand** offers some basic menu items.

NORTH YOSEMITE

On Evergreen Road toward Hetch Hetchy, the **Evergreen Lodge** serves simple and tasty dishes seven nights a week, plus breakfast on weekends from April to October (moderate to expensive). Call (209) 379-2606 for reservations. The **White Wolf Lodge** has fireside breakfasts and dinners (moderate to expensive), and an outdoor patio. Dinner reservations are recommended. Call (209) 372-1316. Of the five High Sierra Camps in the park, **Tuolumne Meadows Lodge** is the only one accessible by car. The dining room is in a tent-like structure, but breakfasts and dinners are first-class. Box lunches are available upon request. Call (209) 372-1313 for required reservations. For reasonably-priced high country chow, the **Tuolumne Meadows Grill** serves it up hot for breakfast, lunch, dinner, and orders to go. No reservations are accepted.

Even though it's two miles outside the park, the **Tioga Pass Resort** is legendary to Yosemite visitors. There might be a bit of a wait for the moderately priced, all-day dining, but their homemade pie is worth it. Call (209) 372-4471.

What about dining in one of the nearby towns?

Groveland 49 miles · Lee Vining 74 miles

Buck Meadows 37 miles

El Portal 14 miles

Mariposa 43 miles

Fish Camp 37 miles

YOSEMITE

GROVELAND
(49 miles from the Big Oak Flat Entrance to park):

Hotel Charlotte
Hearty California country food; (209) 962-6455

BUCK MEADOWS
(37 miles from the Big Oak Flat Entrance to park):

Buck Meadows Lodge
Homestyle food, friendly service
(209) 962-5281

Coffee Express
Great homemade pies and sandwiches
(209) 962-7393
Breakfast & lunch only

EL PORTAL
(14 miles from Arch Rock Entrance to park):

Cedar Lodge Restaurant
(209) 379-2612

Yosemite View Lodge Restaurant
(209) 379-2681
(800) 321-5261

MARIPOSA
(43 miles from the Arch Rock Entrance to park):

Happy Burger
Good inexpensive burgers
(209) 966-2719

LEE VINING
(74 miles from the Tioga Entrance to the park):

Nicely's
Family restaurant, coffee shop style
(619) 647-6477

FISH CAMP
(37 miles from the South Entrance to park):

The Narrow Gauge Inn
Rustic and charming, excellent menu
(209) 683-6446
Closed in winter

> # Is there anywhere one can get a nice spot of tea?

Every place has its traditions. At the Ahwahnee hotel, it's tea and cookies, served every afternoon in the Great Lounge from 5 to 5:30 p.m.

It all goes back to Ansel Adams. As a frequent guest of the Ahwahnee, Adams would while away the afternoon hours playing piano in the lounge, attracting the attention of other guests. The hotel staff noticed they had a little audience on their hands, so they decided to serve some tea and cookies to add to the afternoon's entertainment.

Today, hotel guests can sit in the same lounge, sipping on tea and nibbling on cookies as the day winds down. The original piano player is gone, but a gigantic fireplace sets the perfect mood for lounging, reading, and talking to friends in the luxurious setting of the Ahwahnee Hotel.

Where can we pick up picnic supplies?

Yosemite is the ultimate picnic spot. Where you decide to spread your blanket is up to you, but here are your choices for stocking up on the goods. For store phone numbers, refer to the telephone directory on pages 151–155. For picnic spots, refer to the map on the next page.

YOSEMITE VALLEY

The **Village Store** has it all, including a great meat market and fresh produce. It's located at the east end of the Village Mall at bus stop #3. **Degnan's Deli**, west of the Village Store next to the post office, provides a good spread of picnic goodies. **Curry Village Camp Store** is a general store with food and gifts, located next to the Hamburger Deck at Curry Village. **Housekeeping Camp Store**, near shuttle bus stop #12, caters to your picnic needs from spring to fall. If you order the day before, you can get a picnic-to-go from the **Yosemite Lodge Cafeteria**.

SOUTH YOSEMITE

Picnic supplies in south Yosemite can be found at the **Wawona Grocery Store** next to the gas station, north of the Wawona Hotel. **The Pine Tree Market** is in the heart of north Wawona, less than a mile off the main highway on Chilnualna Fall Road.

NORTH YOSEMITE

There's a limited selection of stores in this area, but the **Crane Flat Gas Station and Store** at the intersection of Big Oat Flat and Tioga Roads provides your basic fare and is open year-round. **White Wolf Lodge** has a tiny camp store next to the lodge dining room. **Tuolumne Meadows Store** offers the largest selection of picnic supplies in north Yosemite.

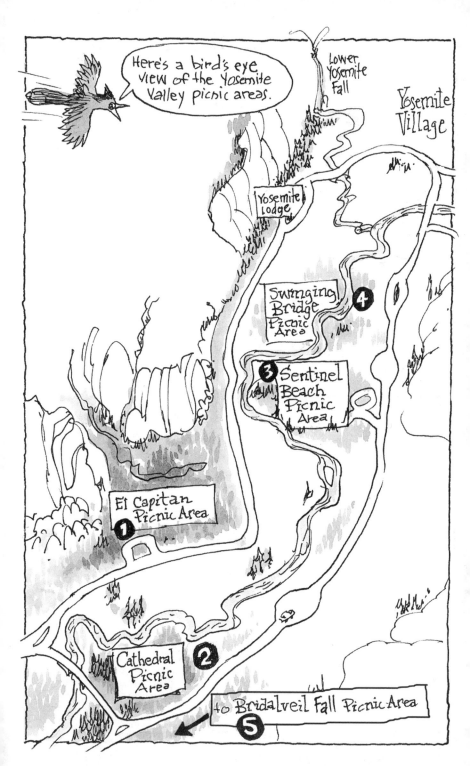

Are there any special seasonal events in Yosemite?

Thanksgiving, New Year's Day, Easter, Valentine's Day—the Ahwahnee hotel celebrates the holidays with amazing spreads of food and drink. One of the classics is the Vintner's Holidays from mid-November to mid-December, when master winemakers gather at the Ahwahnee to host a month-long series of banquets, seminars, and wine tastings. For a fee, you can attend as many events as your taste buds can handle, including the Vintner's Banquet at a cost of $80 per person. Call (209) 252-4848 for more information and reservations for all seasonal feasts.

Oh, if only *I* could go to the Bracebridge Dinner at the Ahwahnee! Every Christmas, the hotel chefs create a multi-course extravaganza, complete with a colorful Yorkshire Christmas pageant. I just haven't been able to get my paws on those high-priced, wait-listed tickets. You should apply through the Yosemite Concession Services (YCS) by January fifteenth. Call (209) 252-4848 for an application, or write to YCS, 5410 E. Home Avenue, Fresno, CA 93727.

As if the Bracebridge Dinner didn't torture me enough, the Ahwahnee follows up with the Chef's Holiday from mid-January to February. Talented chefs are on hand to give demonstrations and prepare five-course feasts for participants. Call (209) 252-4848 to inquire about the Ahwahnee Chef's Package and other events.

V
Camping and Backpacking

What types of campgrounds are available in Yosemite Valley?

There used to be six campgrounds with 779 campsites nestled between the valley's giant towers of granite. The New Year's flood of 1997 changed that configuration to four campgrounds with 418 campsites, all located at the eastern end of the valley at an elevation of four thousand feet. When you camp in the valley, don't expect to be hidden away in the forest far away from other campers. These sites are popular and are always the first to go. Most of them operate on a year-round reservation system.

All the campgrounds are listed below, with helpful information, but here's a quick run-down on the valley camps. Check-in and check-out time is 10 a.m. There aren't any recreational vehicle hook-ups, but there are sanitary dumps. Shower facilities are available from 6 a.m. to 10 p.m. at Curry Village all year, and at Housekeeping Camp starting in late April from 7:30 a.m. to 8 p.m. Starting in early April, Housekeeping Camp also has a laundromat open from 7 a.m. to 7 p.m. Any recycling materials can be cashed in at the Village Store recycling center from noon to 5 p.m., beginning in late April.

Three of the campgrounds are named after the pine trees that shade the eastern end of the valley. **Lower Pines** offers sites near the river and accommodates both RVs and tents. Across the river from Lower Pines sits **North Pines**, open to RVs and tent campers alike. **Upper Pines** is the largest of the valley camps and is the only one open all year. It has a sanitary dump station, welcomes both RVs and tents, and is a pet-friendly campground. All of the Pines' campsites cost $15 per night.

Both the **Upper and Lower River** campgrounds were completely washed away in the New Year flood of 1997.

The **Sunnyside Walk-In** campground, located across from Yosemite Lodge, serves rock climbers and backpackers. All campers carry in their gear and sleep in communal-type sites. Sunnyside operates on a first-come, first-served basis and costs $3 per person.

Backpackers Walk-In is for wilderness permit campers without cars. The campground is accessible only by foot and has a one-night maximum stay. Check-in is at North Pines campground on a first-come, first-served basis.

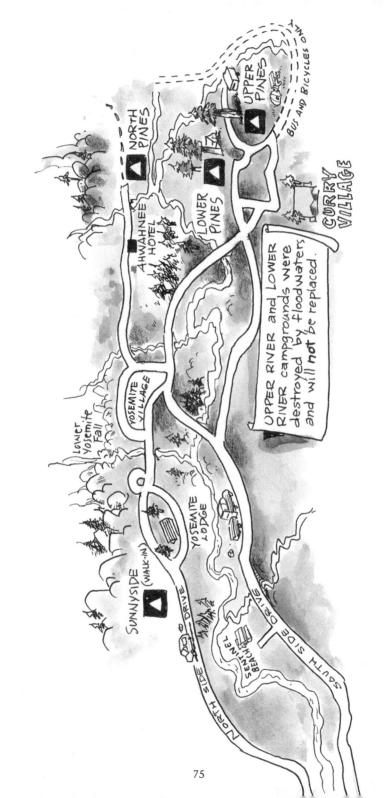

UPPER PINES

NORTH PINES

LOWER PINES

BUS AND BICYCLES ONLY

CURRY VILLAGE

AWAHNEE HOTEL

UPPER RIVER and LOWER RIVER campgrounds were destroyed by floodwaters and will **not** be replaced.

YOSEMITE VILLAGE

Lower Yosemite Fall

YOSEMITE LODGE

SUNNYSIDE (WALK-IN)

NORTH SIDE DRIVE

SENTINEL BEACH

SOUTH SIDE DRIVE

CAMPGROUNDS IN YOSEMITE VALLEY

Campground	Elevation (ft.)	No. of Sites/spaces	Daily Fee**	RV Space	Tent Space	Tap Water	Stream Water (BOIL)	Flush Toilets	Pit Toilets	Tables	Fire Pits or Grill	Pets Allowed	Dump Station	Parking	Showers Nearby	Laundry Nearby	Groceries	Swimming	Fishing	Horseback Riding	Notes
Lower Pines	4000	69	$15/s	•	•		•	•		•	•		•	•	•	•	•	•	•	•	Open All Year Reservations Required
North Pines	4000	85	$15/s	•	•		•	•		•	•		•	•	•	•	•	•	•	•	Open April–November* Reservations Required
Upper Pines	4000	238	$15/s	•	•			•		•	•	•	•	•	•	•	•	•	•	•	Open April–October* Reservations Required
Sunnyside Walk-in	4000	35	$3/p		•		•	•		•	•	•		•	•	•	•	•	•	•	Open All Year/Walk-In First-come, first-served Limited parking available

* Dates approximate
**/s = per site
/p = per person

76

What are the campgrounds outside the valley?

Yosemite Valley may be the heart of the action for visitors, but campers will actually find more campgrounds outside the valley. There are nine total, and even though they're not as busy as the valley camps, they do fill up most summer nights. Arrive early to take advantage of the first-come, first-served system (check-in and check-out time is 12 noon for all campgrounds). A tip for RVs: the only sanitary dumping stations outside the valley are found during the summer at Wawona and Tuolumne Meadows.

SOUTH YOSEMITE

The **Wawona campground** sits on the banks of the Merced River's South Fork, twenty-five miles from the valley at an elevation of four thousand feet. Campsites are open all year, and if winter is your camping season, prepare for snowy conditions. Nine miles out on Glacier Point Road, you'll come across the **Bridalveil Creek** campground. The elevation here is seven thousand feet, so you can count on cooler temperatures year round.

Parts of the Wawona and Bridalveil Creek campgrounds are reserved for group use only. Wawona has also made space for a horse camp. You'll need to make reservations with Biospherics (800/436-PARK [7275]).

NORTH YOSEMITE

The park's northern region offers an all-around rougher brand of camping, with higher elevations, smaller campgrounds, and fewer services. **Tuolumne Meadows** campground is the exception; it's the largest campground in Yosemite, with tons of activities for families. There's also a **Tuolumne group campground**. Call Biospherics for reservations (800/436-PARK [7275]).

Campers with pets are welcome in most north Yosemite campgrounds, including **Crane Flat campground**, located at the intersection of Big Oat Flat and Tioga Road, just seventeen miles away from the valley. If you're driving in from the west on Highway 120, the first camp you'll see is **Hodgdon Meadow campground**, which allows pets and from May to October requires reservations. Call Biospherics (800/436-PARK [7275]). The newest one is **Hetch Hetchy Backpacker's campground**, located at Hetch Hetchy Reservoir, which also has sites for groups and stock use (pets, RVs, and trailers not allowed; wilderness permit required). Along the Tioga Road, there are a number of rustic campgrounds where you don't need a reservation and where you can really rough it, including **Tamarack Flat**, **White Wolf**, **Yosemite Creek**, and **Porcupine Flat**. White Wolf offers the most services, with a lodge, small store, and restaurant. Call (209) 372-0265 weekdays, 9–12 and 1–5, for more information on these campgrounds.

U.S. FOREST SERVICE CAMPGROUNDS OUTSIDE YOSEMITE

For information on the United States Forest Service campgrounds near Yosemite in the Inyo, Sierra, and Stanislaus National Forests, call the following offices: Groveland Ranger Station (Highway 120 West to Stanislaus N.F.), (209) 962-7825; Mono Lake Ranger Station (Highway 120 East to Inyo N.F.), (619) 647-3000; Mariposa Ranger Station (Highway 140 to Sierra N.F.), (209) 966-3638; Oakhurst Ranger Station (Highway 41 to Sierra N.F.), (209) 683-4665.

CAMPGROUNDS OUTSIDE YOSEMITE VALLEY

Campground	Elevation (ft.)	Miles from Yosemite Valley	No. of Sites/spaces	Daily fee**	RV Space	Tent Space	Tap Water	Stream Water (BOIL)	Flush Toilets	Pit Toilets	Tables	Fire Pits or Grill	Pets Allowed	Dump Station	Parking	Showers Nearby	Laundry Nearby	Groceries	Swimming	Fishing	Horseback Riding	Notes
Wawona Hwy 41 in Wawona	4000	27	100	$15/s	•	•	•		•		•	•	•	•	•		•	•	•	•	•	Open All Year *First-come, first-served*
Bridalveil Creek Glacier Point Road	7200	25	110	$10/s	•	•	•		•		•	•	•		•					•		Open June–September* *First-come, first-served*
Tuolumne Meadows Highway 120 East	8600	55	314	$15/s	•	•	•		•		•	•	•	•	•			•		•	•	Open mid-June–Sept.* *1/2 advanced reservations, 1/2 same day reservations, 25 walk-in spaces available for backpackers/visitors without vehicles.*
Crane Flat Hwy. 120 near the Tioga Rd. turnoff	6191	17	166	$15	•	•	•		•		•	•	•		•			•				Open June–October* *Reservations Required*
Hodgdon Meadow Hwy 120 West near Big Oak Flat Entrance	4872	25	105	$15	•	•	•		•		•	•	•		•							Open All Year *Reservations Required approx. May–Oct. First-come, first-served rest of year.*
Tamarack Flat Highway 120 East	6315	23	52	$6/s		•		•		•	•	•	•		•							Open July–early Sept.* *Three-mile access road not suitable for large RV's or trailers.*
White Wolf Highway 120 East	8000	31	87	$10/s	•	•	•		•		•	•	•		•					•		Open July–early Sept.* *First-come, first-served*
Yosemite Creek Highway 120 East	7659	35	75	$6/s		•		•		•	•	•	•		•					•		Open July–early Sept.* *First-come, first-served. Five-mile access road not suitable for large RV's or trailers.*
Porcupine Flat Highway 120 East	8100	38	52	$6/s	•	•		•		•	•	•	•		•							Open July–early Sept.* *RV access front section only.*

* Dates approximate
**/s = per site

Yosemite has 1479 campsites and four million visitors a year. Reservations are required for Yosemite Valley's auto campgrounds year-round, and from summer to fall for Wawona, Hodgdon Meadow, Crane Flat, and half of Tuolumne Meadows' campgrounds. All other campgrounds are available on a first-come, first-served basis (except for group campgrounds). You can register for vacant campsites starting at 7:30 a.m. with a ranger, or self-register by following the posted instructions. A tip: the campgrounds along Tioga Road are last to fill up.

All reservations can be made through the central reservations system, Biospherics (800/436-PARK [7275]). For 1998, here's the schedule for booking campground reservations:

CAMPING ARRIVAL DATE	FIRST DAY TO RESERVE
3/15/98–6/14/98	3/15/98
4/15/98–7/14/98	4/15/98
5/15/98–8/14/98	5/15/98
6/15/98–9/14/98	6/15/98
7/15/98–10/14/98	7/15/98
8/15/98–11/14/98	8/15/98
9/15/98–12/14/98	9/15/98
10/15/98–1/14/99	10/15/98
11/15/98–2/14/99	11/15/98
12/15/98–3/14/99	12/15/98

After 1998, call Biospherics for any reservation schedule changes.

For our summer season, campers should call Biospherics as early as possible at (800) 436-PARK or (800) 436-7275. International callers dial 1 (301) 722-1257. You can place your call starting at 7 a.m. Pacific Time. You can also mail in a reservation request form (see page 148) to National Park Reservation Service (NPRS), P. O. Box 1600, Cumberland, Maryland 21502—but you must call in your reservation to Biospherics first. Reservations for Wawona and Bridalveil Creek group camps can also be mailed to NPRS, no sooner than twelve weeks in advance. You can pay with Visa, Mastercard, Discover, or personal check.

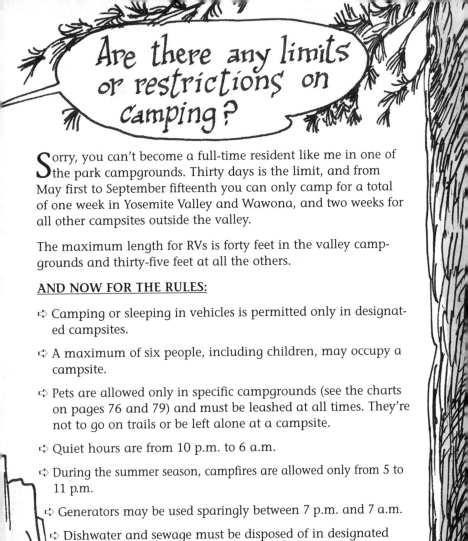

Are there any limits or restrictions on camping?

Sorry, you can't become a full-time resident like me in one of the park campgrounds. Thirty days is the limit, and from May first to September fifteenth you can only camp for a total of one week in Yosemite Valley and Wawona, and two weeks for all other campsites outside the valley.

The maximum length for RVs is forty feet in the valley campgrounds and thirty-five feet at all the others.

AND NOW FOR THE RULES:

⇨ Camping or sleeping in vehicles is permitted only in designated campsites.

⇨ A maximum of six people, including children, may occupy a campsite.

⇨ Pets are allowed only in specific campgrounds (see the charts on pages 76 and 79) and must be leashed at all times. They're not to go on trails or be left alone at a campsite.

⇨ Quiet hours are from 10 p.m. to 6 a.m.

⇨ During the summer season, campfires are allowed only from 5 to 11 p.m.

⇨ Generators may be used sparingly between 7 p.m. and 7 a.m.

⇨ Dishwater and sewage must be disposed of in designated utility drains.

⇨ Electrical extension cords cannot be connected to restroom outlets.

Well, we got that out of the way. Now let's go camping!

Can we build a campfire?

The campfire's comforting crackle is one of the best parts of camping, but it has also caused some of our air quality problems and forest fires. As long as you follow a few guidelines, our next generation of campers can enjoy fireside gatherings as well.

Start by using established campfire rings, then check around the area for potential spark hazards. Never leave fires unattended; put them out by stirring in water before you leave the campground, and do a final check for any remaining embers. Remember, during the summer camp season, fires are only allowed from 5 to 11 p.m. With a wilderness permit, you can have a campfire in the backcountry below ninety-six hundred feet in elevation. The sequoia groves, however, are strict no-fire zones.

If you're using a portable camping stove, refuel it only when it's cold and in a well-ventilated area. Keep any burning charcoals out of tents and vehicles, and douse the coals with water when you're finished.

To fuel your fires, you can bring firewood from home or buy some in the stores both in and out of the valley. Gathering wood is an option outside the valley and sequoia groves, as long as the wood is dead and on the ground. If you try to collect some wood or pine cones in Yosemite Valley or sequoia groves, you might also collect a $50 to $100 citation.

Not with wet wood!

Where can we rent camping gear and buy supplies inside the park?

You're better off renting gear before you arrive in Yosemite. The same equipment will probably cost more in the park, and, frankly, there just isn't much gear to rent here—not even tents. Sleeping bags and foam pads are sometimes available through the Yosemite Mountaineering School, but during the summer months most of their equipment is reserved for the school's group trips. The school moves around during the course of the year, and shuts down in really bad weather. Give them a call at (209) 372-8344 (winter) or (209) 372-8435 (summer) for prices and more information.

You can buy propane fuel at the Tuolumne Meadows Gas Station from 9 a.m. to 6 p.m. (summers only) and in Wawona year-round. Call (209) 372-1000 for the valley location. Food supplies are purchased in various stores throughout the park (see page 70).

Wherever you get your camp stuff, here's a short list of essentials: Tent with rainfly, ground cloth, warm sleeping bag, sleeping pad, flashlight, food, cooking stove and fuel, and any personal gear. If you're going to stay at our High Sierra Camps, you might want to pick up travel sheets (13.4 oz.); they're not provided at the camps.

84

What are the High Sierra Camps like?

Hikers return year after year to Yosemite's five High Sierra Camps, located at intervals of five and a half to ten miles along a loop trail at elevations of seventy-two hundred to around ten thousand feet. From June to September, each camp offers its own spectacular setting, rustic accommodations, helpful staff, and hearty meals. Unfortunately, youngsters under age seven aren't allowed.

Men and women stay in separate dormitory-style tent cabin, with wood-burning stoves (except at Merced Lake), tables and chairs, candles, and hooks and shelves for gear. Beds are outfitted with mattresses, pillows, woolen blankets, and comforters. Hikers can even receive the warm welcome of a hot shower, though sometimes usage is limited.

Breakfasts and dinners are prepared by the camp staff and served in generous portions, and picnic lunches are available upon request. The cost is around $90 per night for lodging, breakfast, dinner, and showers. Those of you who are camping on your own can opt for dinners and breakfasts only for $26 per day, or the box lunch at $6.50.

Due to high demand and limited space, reservations are granted by lottery. You can submit a High Sierra Camp lottery application form to Yosemite Reservations between October 15 and November 30. Applications prior to and after these dates aren't accepted, and remember, only one application per party. The lottery is held in mid-December, and spaces are divvied up by the end of March. Cancellations are filled by waiting list until May 1, then it's telephone inquiry time. For more information or to request a lottery application, call the High Sierra Desk at (209) 253-5674.

Unfortunately... children under seven and bears aren't allowed.

What is Yosemite's backcountry wilderness like?

"**B**ackcountry" means an area that's reached only by foot or on horseback. In 1984, the U.S. Congress designated almost the entire Yosemite region as wilderness area—all but six percent of it. That means there's plenty of opportunity to lose the crowds and wander into some of the world's most breathtaking scenery.

But don't forget the "wild" part of wilderness; out here, weather and trail conditions can change quickly. At seven thousand to eleven thousand feet, your dusty trail can turn into a snow-covered path faster than you can say "did we pack our snow shoes?" During spring and early summer, winter's runoff can fill the rivers and streams to dangerous levels. Any crossing, with or without a bridge, should be taken with caution.

Hiking the backcountry in fall is like walking under a waterfall of autumn color. It's also a time of unpredictable weather, like the snow-storm that pelted us one September. Expect freezing temperatures at night, and be prepared for sudden storms.

Winter's white cover doesn't mean the backcountry is off limits, it just means you have to trade in your boots for cross-country skis or snow-shoes. Both groomed and ungroomed trails cross expanses of wilderness to places like Glacier Point, Crane Flat, and the south rim of the valley. For more information, call (209) 372-0740 to reach the Yosemite Wilderness Center, or (209) 372-0265 for trail conditions.

HERE'S A SAMPLING OF WHAT YOU'LL FIND IN THE PARK'S BACKCOUNTRY REGIONS:

The canyons in the northern and western regions of Yosemite contain some of the most beautiful country in the Sierra Nevada.

The Hetch Hetchy area between Highway 120 and the Tuolumne River hosts a large variety of elevations and plant life. One of the more popular trails here rises more than ten thousand feet to the summit of Mt. Hoffman.

Tuolumne Meadows trails (north of Highway 120) wind through a subalpine world of jagged peaks, crystal-clear lakes, glaciated domes, and roaring cascades. The sights here match any visitor's greatest expectations.

The Tuolumne Meadows trails south and east of Highway 120 are used frequently, so reserve your space with a wilderness permit before you embark. They're popular for good reason: these paths take you past spectacular passes and mountain lakes.

Yosemite Valley is a safe option, providing a rich array of history and scenery on many different trails.

Glacier Point offers cooler temperatures than you'll find in Wawona or Yosemite Valley, with elevations ranging between six and seven thousand feet. There are fewer and less-used trails here, with amazing views, that take you to the edge of Yosemite Valley or on longer excursions through a variety of mountain life zones.

Yosemite's southeastern backcountry has the highest trail point in the entire park, and the journey there is filled with green havens of lodgepole pines and unique, subalpine regions.

Are there any organized hiking trips into Yosemite's wilderness?

One of the best ways to see our backcountry is on a seven-day hike led by a naturalist from the Yosemite Association. The trip starts at the Tuolumne Meadows Lodge and stops overnight at each of the five High Sierra Camps and two nights at Merced Lake. You need to be in good shape for these treks, as they can cover up to ten miles each day and climb up to over ten thousand feet at some locations. Before starting the journey, you should spend a day around Tuolumne Meadows to acclimate to the higher elevations.

The price (subject to change) is approximately $735 per person for six nights' lodging and all meals at the High Sierra Camps. Weather permitting, the hikes usually depart two days a week, from late June to early September. Children under age twelve are not permitted, and anyone under age eighteen must be accompanied by an adult. For more information and reservations, call the High Sierra desk at (209) 253-5674. You can also check out the Yosemite Association's Field Seminar Program (see Educational Programs in this book's Quick Reference section). Yosemite Concession Services also offers a guided backpacking program during the summer out of Tuolumne Meadows Mountaineering School. Call the school at (209) 372-8435.

You may want to explore the backcountry on horseback or by hiking next to a pack animal. These custom trips require a minimum of three pack and/or saddle animals, and each group must be accompanied by a guide. Trips range from a day to a week, with no more than 150 pounds per pack animal and 225 pounds per saddle animal. For more information, call the Tuolumne Stables at (209) 372-8427 (summer only).

A little less organized please.

When and why do we need wilderness permits?

Wilderness permits are required when you plan to camp in the wilderness. No problem—they're free, and they cut down on overcrowding during peak season by limiting the number of campers in the areas. During the winter, permits provide important safety information and also help rangers keep track of whoever is exploring around the area. Permits are not required for day hikes.

Up to half the number of spaces allowed on a given day can be reserved in advance; the other half are gobbled up on a first-come, first-served basis at the Wilderness Permit Stations the day before or the same day the trip begins.

To reserve your wilderness permit, mail a reservation request letter (see instructions on pg. 163) to Wilderness Reservations, Wilderness Center, P.O. Box 545, Yosemite, CA 95389. Be sure to include a $3 processing fee per person. Checks may be made payable to the Yosemite Association. Requests will be processed twenty-four weeks in advance of the first day of your trip. To reserve by phone, call (209) 372-0740. You can also complete the task in person at the following permit stations: The Wilderness Center in Yosemite Valley, Wawona Ranger Station (summer and fall), Big Oak Flat Information Station (spring, summer, and fall), and Tuolumne Meadows Wilderness Permit Station (summer only). For wilderness information, call (209) 372-0200.

What should we know about camping and backpacking in Yosemite's backcountry?

A wilderness excursion is a bit different than a stroll through Yosemite Village. You should check on weather conditions before you embark, and be prepared for the possibility that the forecast is completely wrong. Hiking the backcountry requires an ample amount of time for rest and searching for that perfect campsite. Park regulations say you must be four trail miles from Yosemite Valley, Tuolumne Meadows, or Wawona and a mile from any road while camping, and in groups of no more than fifteen people on the trails and eight for off-trail hikes. Our wilderness area is a wildlife preserve; that means no pets, weapons, bicycles, or strollers. You can stay a maximum of thirty days in the backcountry, and it's a good idea to let friends and family know your itinerary.

HERE ARE A FEW RULES OF THUMB TO REMEMBER:

Be extra careful crossing streams during spring runoff.

Pack out all trash.

Use gas stoves instead of firewood.

Protect yourself and the wildlife by using proper food storage containers (see page 92).

Protect fragile areas and water quality by choosing existing, well-used campsites at least one hundred feet from water.

Purify all drinking water by boiling three to five minutes, or with Giardia-rated filters or iodine-based chemical treatment.

Protect water quality by disposing human waste in small holes at least one hundred feet from water and by doing all washing at similar distances from water sources.

Abiding by these rules will enhance your backcountry experience and help preserve Yosemite's natural heritage. For more wilderness information, call (209) 372-0265 for trail conditions.

BEAR FACTS AND AMAZING BEAR TRICKS

- The last Grizzly bear was killed in Yosemite in 1895. The black bear is the only species left in the park.

- Yosemite's black bears can be a variety of colors including brown, blonde, cinnamon, or black.

- Yosemite black bears can range in size from 250 to 500 pounds. These are omnivores and will eat almost anything including insects, small rodents, berries, acorns, seeds, and human food.

- Many of the black bears go into a den in the winter months for a sleep that is not a true hibernation. The young cubs are born in late winter and come out of the den in spring to forage for food with their mother.

- Bears in Yosemite have figured out how to get garbage out of "bear-proof" dumpsters by laying down on the hinged top door, causing it to close. Then by keeping one leg outside, they hang upside down inside the dumpster, grab the garbage, and pull themselves back out.

- Bears have figured out several ways to get the food bags that campers hang from trees. A sow will sometimes send one of her cubs up the tree after the food, and some bears will actually chew through the tree limbs to send the food crashing down.

- Some trees have wires between them for hanging food. Bears have been known to shinny out to the middle of the wire, with their weight bending it toward the ground. Then they let go, sling-shooting the food some distance away. All that's left to do is hunt for the food where it landed.

Will we have any problems with bears in the wilderness?

We black bears are curious creatures, and sometimes we'll rummage around people areas in search of accessible food. We've been known to rip open car doors in search of goodies and even freefall from branches to snag the food bags that campers hang from trees. Both people and bears have been injured and too many of my friends and relatives have been killed as a result. You can help save both our hides by following some simple suggestions.

Store all food, including supplies like ice chests and cans, in metal storage boxes where provided, and use clips to secure these boxes. Any grocery bags, garbage, and other scented items like soap, sunscreen, and toothpaste should be stored as well. Airtight containers will supply that extra bit of prevention.

When storage boxes are not available, put all food and supplies in your car trunk.

If you don't have a trunk, you still have to get that stuff out of sight. Cover it up in your car with tarps or blankets and close the windows.

Food should be stored day and night. We bears have been known to take midday strolls through campgrounds and picnic areas.

Keep your campsite clean by putting trash in bear-proof cans and dumpsters.

While you're out on day hikes, store all food supplies at the trail-head, either in your car trunk or in lockers, or keep it with you at all times while hiking.

Don't leave your backpack lying around. Bears think packs are giftwrapped food.

In the backcountry, plan ahead to store your food by renting ($3 per night) or buying ($75) bear-proof food canisters, available at the Yosemite Valley Sports Shop, the Yosemite Valley Wilderness Center, Curry Village Mountain Shop, Crane Flat Grocery, Wawona Store, and Tuolumne Meadows Sport Shop.

If you're staying in hard-sided cabins or rooms, keep your supplies indoors.

In canvas tent-cabins, all foodlike bear magnets must be kept in lock-ers, when available, or stored properly in cars.

With all these precautions, you might have already figured out the most important one: never approach a bear, especially cubs. There are approximately three bears for every two square miles, and if you come across one of us, clap your hands, yell, bang pots together, whatever you can do to seem bigger and badder. After any bear encounter, report it to the nearest ranger. One more hint: if a bear already has your backpack in its paws, let it go, because hey, that backpack is *gone*.

Almost every technique and piece of equipment used by rock climbers around the world was either developed or perfected at Yosemite National Park, such as:

- 1940s to 1960s — Stove leg pitons (actual legs from stoves) were first used and later refined during ascents of El Capitan.

- 1950s to 1980s — The big wall technique was developed here and used in the first ascent of El Capitan in 1958 and other subsequent Yosemite climbs.

- 1970s–1980s — The use and development of artificial nuts and wedges made of aluminum in Yosemite has contributed to a new "clean climbing" ethic in the sport.

- 1980s to present — The use of spring-loaded cams and other mechanical protection devices was refined at Yosemite.

- The development and refinement of crack-climbing techniques has allowed climbers to scale 5.12 cracks in Yosemite.

- Some of the sport's most noteworthy free-soloing climbs have taken place in Yosemite including "Astroman" on Washington Column and "The Rostrum" in the Merced River Canyon.

- Sunnyside Campground, or Camp Four, in Yosemite has some of the most famous and most difficult "boulder problems" (short climbs of thirty feet or less without ropes) in the world, including "Midnight Lighting" and "Thriller."

VI
Recreational Opportunities

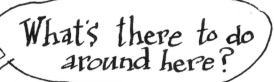

What's there to do around here?

When you first enter Yosemite, you're sure to be overwhelmed by how big it is. You'll wish you had wings so you could take it all in. Well, there are plenty of year-round activities that allow you to experience the best the park has to offer.

A journey on our eight hundred miles of walking trails begins with a single step. From steep, lofty hikes to mellow strolls on the valley floor, these many paths take you through Yosemite's most spectacular landscapes.

For a swifter route, we have eight miles of bike trails winding through the valley. Weather permitting, you can rent bikes year-round and pedal your way past meadows and along the river to famous vistas of Half Dome and El Capitan—but stick to the paved bike trails and roads.

After a hot summer day on the trails, a great way to cool down is to take a plunge into cool waters. There are plenty of good swimming holes along the sandy beaches of the Merced River at the eastern end of the valley, or higher up among the lakes, creeks, and rivers of northern Yosemite; but be careful of the chilly, swift currents. You could also try the calmer waters in the swimming pools at Yosemite Lodge, Curry Village, or as a guest at the Ahwahnee or Wawona Hotels.

In the summer, rafting the Merced River is a fun and relaxing way to explore the valley. If sailing is your choice, the afternoon winds on Tenaya Lake provide the perfect fuel for sailboats and windsurfers (motor boats not permitted).

You don't have to go far to cast a line in Yosemite waters: we have 880 miles of rivers and streams and 127 stocked lakes and reservoirs.

On horseback, you can tour the high country (summers only), trying the same mode of travel as Yosemite's native peoples and pioneers.

After watching rock climbers tackle the challenging granite faces, you might be tempted to give it a shot yourself. The Yosemite Mountaineering School is one of the best at teaching basic technique and proper equipment use. The school also offers intermediate and advanced lessons.

Some people might ask, "why ruin a perfectly nice walk in the park," but we do have a great nine-hole golf course next to the Wawona Hotel.

One of the park's best-kept secrets is the wide range of activities found in winter. That's when you can downhill ski at Badger Pass, ice-skate at Curry Village, cross-country ski some of our ninety miles of trails, or take a ranger-led snowshoe tour. Educational activities are also available through the Yosemite Association's Field Seminar Programs and the National Park Service's Junior Snow Ranger program for children.

How much of the park is accessible to hikers?

The entire park is accessible to hikers, but unless you have the survival instincts of a bear, you have to be an expert with a map and compass to travel off-trail. When you hike the trails in Yosemite, you're carrying on a tradition that goes back hundreds, even thousands, of years. These trails—trekked by Indians, pioneers, and generations of backpackers and hikers—are your best shot at getting an insider's look at Yosemite.

YOSEMITE VALLEY
You can cover much of the valley with easy hikes to Mirror Lake, Vernal Fall Bridge and Lower Yosemite Fall and with tougher treks to the valley's rim via Yosemite Falls Trail, the Four-Mile Trail (summer), Snow Creek Trail, and the Vernal and Nevada Falls Trail (summer). Any one you choose will provide spectacular vistas of the area. As rewarding as the demanding trail to the summit of Half Dome can be, plan this trip only for sometime between late May and early October.

SOUTH YOSEMITE
Wawona is the starting point for many great hikes, and it's less crowded than the valley. You can start with the easy route along Meadow Loop, then try the tougher Chilnualna Fall trail or the hike to Mariposa Big Trees (or, consider taking the free shuttle from Wawona to the Mariposa Grove and walking *downhill* to Wawona!). Higher up are the trails starting from Glacier Point Road, including the popular Panorama and Pohona Day Trails and the short hikes to Taft Point, Sentinel Dome, and Mono Meadow. For wilderness excursions, the Glacier Point Road trails lead to the Clark Range and the southern portion of the park. Once you're in the Mariposa Grove, try the easy walks to the Grizzly Giant or Wawona Point.

NORTH YOSEMITE

Hetch Hetchy reservoir, located in the northwest part of the park, is at the same elevation as the valley, but it's usually much warmer. In winter this is a good starting point for day hikes such as the main trail from the reservoir at the top of the dam, which will take you past some awesome falls. Summer and fall are the times to tackle the trails along Tioga Road, including the easy hike to Tuolomne Meadows, the moderate hikes to Harden and Lukens Lakes, and the challenging thirteen-mile hike down to the valley, or the tough treks up to North Dome, May and Gaylor Lakes, and Mono Pass. The high country trails around Tuolumne Meadows offer cooler temperatures and smaller crowds. From here, eight different trailheads lead back-packers and day hikers into a range of wilderness adventures.

FIRE FACTS

- Between 1931 and 1996, there were over twenty-seven hundred natural fires caused by lightning in Yosemite, an average of forty-three natural fires a year.

- Since 1972, natural fires have burned an average of twenty-four hundred acres a year in Yosemite's wilderness.

- Since 1970, staff-controlled prescribed burns have torched an average of thirteen hundred acres a year in Yosemite's lower elevations.

- If you see smoke while you're in the park it could be:

  ⇨ a prescribed fire set by National Park Service rangers under proper conditions to help keep the park's forests and meadows ecologically healthy and to restore natural conditions; or

  ⇨ a prescribed natural fire caused by lightning. These fires are allowed to burn without intervention in areas full of dead and down fuel—and where there's no threat to property or human lives.

What should we take on our day hike?

You won't get far without a sturdy pair of sneakers or boots, and you'll wish you hadn't gone so far if the weather changes and you're caught without an extra layer of clothing and a rainproof shell. Sometimes a hike lasts longer than you expect; instead of having to find your way back in the dark, pack a flashlight.

Plenty of water is an essential, especially in hot weather and on difficult hikes. It's a good idea to bring snacks, particularly with children along. Once kids become hungry and thirsty, it doesn't matter how blue the lake is or how colorful the wildflowers are, they want to go home. Some favorite snacks for hikers of all ages are granola bars, popcorn, dried and fresh fruit, and trail mix. Whatever you bring, remember to pack out your trash.

Once you're away from the visitor areas, your only bathroom convenience is the toilet paper you carry with you. Human waste must be buried at least six inches deep, one hundred feet or more from any water and trails.

A compact first-aid kit or even a few bandages will take care of any cuts and scrapes. Before you embark on your hikes, you'd be smart to apply lip balm, insect repellent, and sunscreen.

Depending on your interests, you can bring other items along that will make your adventures more interesting, such as field books, binoculars, a camera, and fishing gear. If you plan on going off-trail, a map and compass and the know-how to use them are vital tools.

I keep thinking we forgot somethin'

100

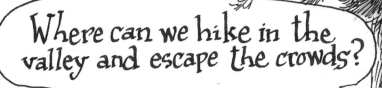

Where can we hike in the valley and escape the crowds?

Believe it or not, there are places to hike in the valley where you won't be one of thousands of people. They're not exactly secret spots, but they're less crowded than are most popular hikes to Happy Isles, the Vernal Fall Bridge, Nevada Fall's brink, and the bases of Yosemite and Bridalveil Fall. In winter, even these hot spots are uncrowded, and with the valley's lower elevation, you won't need a pair of snowshoes to get around. In the first month of spring, the waterfalls are gushing but the people-traffic is only a trickle (except on weekends). Same goes for the fall, when smaller audiences get to see the brilliant show of changing colors.

Then there's late spring and summer, when flash floods of visitors roar into the valley. If you want to avoid being swept away, there are some options. While most visitors are near the visitor facilities to the east of Yosemite Lodge, you can head west to escape the crowds and wander through some of the valley's best scenery. Most of these trails are level hikes, which lead along the Merced River, past forests, meadows, and wildflower havens. I suggest the Sentinel/Cook's Meadow (seven and a half miles) and the El Capitan/Pohono Bridge/Bridalveil (six miles) loop trails. There's no shuttle service west of the lodge, so you should leave a pick-up car if you head out on a long one-way trail.

One last tip: weekdays and early mornings are less crowded hiking times in every season.

We'd like an easy day hike. Any suggestions?

If you're looking for an easy trail that takes no more than two and a half to three hours, the following chart will give you some suggestions. These popular hikes follow along flat trails that won't wipe you out for the rest of the day. The trailheads are easy to find, with scenic photo spots of famous sights, picnic areas, and plenty of ways to hop onto other good trails. All of them are good hikes for families with children, and some have the added bonus of a place to swim and fish. Be prepared for lots of company on these routes, as many visitors will be following the same paths.

HIKE	TIME	DISTANCE	DIFFICULTY	STARTS FROM
Yosemite Valley				
Bridalveil Fall	20 min. rt	.5 mile	easy	Bridalveil Fall lot
Camp Curry Loop	2 hrs.	2.8 miles	easy	Camp Curry
Happy Isles	20 min. rt	.5 mile	easy	Happy Isles
Lower Yosemite Fall	20 min. rt	.5 mile	easy	Yosemite Falls lot
Mirror Lake/Meadow	1 hr. rt to lake	1.0 mile	easy	Mirror Lake shuttle stop
	2 hour loop	3.0 miles	easy	Mirror Lake shuttle stop
Vernal Fall Bridge	1 hr. rt	.8 mile	easy	Happy Isles
Yosemite Valley Loop	2 hrs.	2.8 miles	easy	Sentinel Bridge lot
Yosemite Village Loop	2 hrs.	3.3 miles	easy	Yosemite Falls lot
South Yosemite				
Grizzly Giant	1 hr. rt	.8 mile	easy	Mariposa Grove
Sentinel Dome	2 hrs. rt	2.2 miles	easy	Glacier Point Road
Taft Point	2 hrs. rt	2.2 miles	easy	Glacier Point Road
Wawona Meadow Loop	2.5 hrs.	3.0 miles	easy	Wawona
Wawona Point	45 min. rt	1.0 mile	easy	Mariposa Grove
North Yosemite				
Pothole Dome	1 hr. rt	.5 mile	easy	Tuolumne Meadows
Soda Springs	1 hr. rt	1.5 miles	easy	Tuolumne Meadows
Tenaya Lake Loop	2 hrs.	3.1 miles	easy	Highway 120
Tuolumne Meadows	1 hr. rt	1.5 miles	easy	Tioga Road

NOTE:
rt . . . . **round trip**

These trails are a bit tougher than the easy hikes, requiring more time and a little more oomph to walk up some moderate slopes and occasional steep parts. Families with children are welcome to have a go; just make sure you have plenty of water and snacks. Many of these treks will lead you to great picnicking spots, awesome scenery, points of historic buildings, and lakes to fish and swim in during the summer months.

HIKE	TIME	DISTANCE	DIFFICULTY	STARTS FROM
Yosemite Valley				
Mirror Lake Loop	4 hrs.	4.8 miles	moderate	Mirror Lake shuttle stop
Tenaya Canyon Loop	4–6 hrs.	6.6 miles	moderate	Valley stables
Vernal Fall (top)	3–4 hrs. rt	4.6 miles	moderate +	Happy Isles
West Valley Loop	3.5 hrs.	4.0 miles	moderate	Devil's Elbow picnic area
South Yosemite				
Dewey Point	4–6 hrs. rt	7.0 miles	moderate	Glacier Point Road
Four Mile Trail to Yosemite Valley	3–4 hrs.	4.5 miles	moderate	Glacier Point Road
Mariposa Grove	4–5 hrs. rt	6.3 miles	moderate	Mariposa Grove
McGurk's Meadow and Bridalveil Creek	3.5 hrs. rt	4.0 miles	moderate	Glacier Point Road
Mono Meadow and Mt. Starr King View	3 hrs. rt	3.0 miles	moderate	Glacier Point Road
Wawona Tunnel Tree down to Mariposa Grove	2–3 hrs.	2.5 miles	moderate	Mariposa Grove
North Yosemite				
Cascade Creek	3.5 hrs. rt	5.0 miles	moderate	Tioga Road
Dog Lake	4 hrs. rt	3.0 miles	moderate	Tuolumne Meadows
Elizabeth Lake	3.5 hrs. rt	4.6 miles	moderate +	Tioga Road
Harden Lake	4 hrs. rt	5.0 miles	moderate	White Wolf
Lembert Dome	3 hrs. rt	2.8 miles	moderate +	Tioga Road
Lukens Lake I	3 hrs. rt	4.6 miles	moderate	White Wolf
Lukens Lake II	1 hr. rt	1.6 miles	moderate	Tioga Road
Lyell Canyon	4 hrs. + rt	6–14 miles	moderate	Tioga Road
May Lake	2 hrs. rt	2.4 miles	moderate	Tioga Road
Merced Grove of Sequoia	3 hrs. rt	4.0 miles	moderate	Big Oak Flat
Wapama Falls	3.5 hrs. rt	4.0 miles	moderate	Evergreen

NOTE:
rt . . . .**round trip**
+ . . . .**more difficult/more time**

What are some great butt-kicking hikes?

For those who like to get their hearts really pumping and feel the burn in their legs, here's a list of some wilderness and high country trails that will happily oblige. You'll need to be in good shape and carefully plan your trip for these babies, but they'll pay you back with great scenery, fewer crowds, and a feeling of accomplishment once you're finished. Most of these can be done in a day, but many of them also have overnight camping areas along the way. Just be sure you have the time and energy before embarking on these journeys, as most of them have strenuous uphill climbs on switchback trails, and the higher elevations mean that much more huffing and puffing.

ARE YOU **SURE** YOU WANT TO DO THIS?

HIKE	TIME	DISTANCE	DIFFICULTY	STARTS FROM
Yosemite Valley				
Four Mile Trail to Glacier Point	6–8 hrs. rt	9.6 miles	strenuous ++	Southside Drive
Half Dome	10–12 hrs. rt	16.4 miles	strenuous	Happy Isles
Tenaya Canyon/Snow Creek Trail to North Dome	8–10 hrs. rt	19.2 miles	strenuous ++	Mirror Lake
Vernal and Nevada Falls	4–6 hrs. rt	5.9 miles	strenuous	Happy Isles
Yosemite Falls	6–8 hrs. rt	7.0 miles	strenuous	Yosemite Falls Lot
South Yosemite				
Chilnualna Fall	6–8 hrs. rt	8.0 miles	strenuous	Wawona
Panorama Trail to Yosemite Valley	6–8 hrs.	8.5 miles	strenuous –	Glacier Point
Wawona Hotel to Mariposa Big Trees	8–10 hrs. rt	13.0 miles	strenuous –	Mariposa Grove
North Yosemite				
Cathedral Lakes	4–6 hrs. rt	7.9 miles	strenuous +	Tuolumne Meadows
Gaylor Lakes	3 hrs. rt	3.0 miles	strenuous	Tioga Road
Glen Aulin and Waterwheel Falls	8–10 hrs. rt	14 .0 miles	strenuous ++	Tuolumne Meadows
May Lake to Mt. Hoffmann	6–8 hrs. rt	6.0 miles	strenuous	Old Tioga Road
Mono Pass	4–6 hrs. rt	4.0 miles	strenuous	Tioga Road
North Dome	6–8 hrs. rt	9.6 miles	strenuous –	Tioga Road
Yosemite Creek to Yosemite Valley	8 hrs.	13 miles	strenuous	Tioga Road

NOTE:

rt ....round trip
+ ....more difficult/more time
++ ....very strenuous
– ....less strenuous

107

Can we mountain bike in Yosemite?

CHECK OUT THE VIEW!

The good news for mountain bikers is that you are allowed on the public roads as well as more than eight miles of biking trails winding through the valley's best scenery. The bad news is, that's it; all hiking trails and meadows are off-limits to two-wheelers. The Glacier Point and Tioga Roads are open to bikers in the summer, as are some roads in Wawona. Call (209) 372-0265 for conditions of the Glacier Point and Tioga Roads. Call the Wawona Information Station, (209) 375-9501, for more information on area roads. If you want to ride off-trail, try some of the dirt roads and trails in the National Forest areas outside the park. For more information, see page 78.

Off-trail riding is barred in Yosemite to protect the vegetation, wildlife, and hikers. Some road use is limited as well, like the paved paths to Mirror Lake and Yosemite Falls, to prevent any collisions with the many folks strolling along.

With the valley's heavy car traffic in summer and early fall, it's a safe bet to keep off the main valley roads with your bike. Try the valley's east end bike paths, where there are no cars and fewer crowds.

BEFORE YOU RIDE OFF INTO THE DISTANCE, THERE ARE A FEW RULES TO KNOW

⇨ Anyone under age eighteen is required to wear a helmet.

⇨ No bikes are allowed on hiking trails or in meadows—a rule which helps prevent erosion and damage to vegetation.

⇨ Ride to the right in single file.

⇨ Rules apply to bikes of every type, including mountain bikes.

Can we rent bikes?

Beach cruisers are available all year at Yosemite Lodge (unless it's snowing, raining, or just too cold to pedal) and at Curry Village during the summer. You can rent bikes by the hour or day, and they'll throw in helmets and locks, free of charge. Child carriers are available (I'm still waiting for the bear seats). Bikes can't be reserved, but don't worry, they never run out of them.

Bikes rent for $5.25 per hour, so if you plan on riding around for four hours or more, you might as well have the bike all day for $20. If you're up for a shorter tour, you can roam all eight miles of bike paths in a couple of hours or less.

The rental shop located in front of the swimming pool at Yosemite Lodge is open daily from 8 a.m. to 7 p.m. in the summer. You can call the shop at (209) 372-1208 for more information. The Curry Village rental office, open 8 a.m. to 6 p.m., is next to the hamburger stand and can be reached at (209) 372-8319 (season closes November 3).

Where can we ski in the park?

No other ski resort in the entire state can make the same claim as Yosemite Park: we have California's first ski area, Badger Pass. This granddaddy of the slopes has been going strong since 1928, and over the years, generations of skiers have learned to downhill, cross-country, and, more recently, snowboard on its friendly terrain. Badger Pass offers a triple-chair lift, three double-chairs, one surface lift, nine ski runs, and ninety miles of cross-country trails through some of the best scenery in the world.

Downhill skiers and snowboarders can receive expert instruction from the Badger Pass ski school as well as rent all the necessary equipment at the local ski shop. For all-day rentals of downhill skis, boots, and poles, it costs $18 for adults and $13 for children age twelve and under. Snowboards and boots run $30 for all-day rentals. Two-hour classes for both skiers and snowboarders cost $22. Lift tickets run $22 for adults midweek and $28 for weekends and holidays. Children's tickets run $13 for a full day and $9 for a half day. Call (209) 372-8430 for more information.

Cross-country skiers receive the same services without having to pay trail fees. Skis, boots, and poles go for $15 for adults and $9 for children age twelve and under. A two-hour lesson costs $20. Of the ninety miles of marked trails, twenty-one miles are smooth, machine-groomed tracks to the Clark Range Vista and Glacier Point. Additional cross-country adventures are found in overnight stays at the Ostrander (209/372-0740) and Glacier Point (209/372-8444) Ski Huts and other guided Trans-Sierra expeditions. Call (209) 372-1000

Well... it *is* called Badger Pass.

WOOOSH!

110

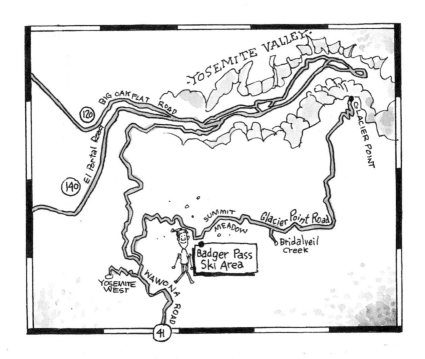

for snow conditions. For more information on cross-country skiing, call (209) 372-8444.

Special Badger Pass ski packages offer midweek (Sunday through Thursday) guests of the Ahwahnee, Yosemite Lodge, and Wawona Hotel free lift tickets from January 1 to March 31 (except holidays). For an extra $25 per person per day, they throw in a couple of down-hill or cross-country lessons, one day of free childcare at the ski area, ice rink passes, and courtesy shuttles to and from Badger Pass. For the same price, toddlers can join the Badger Pups ski school, which includes ski equipment.

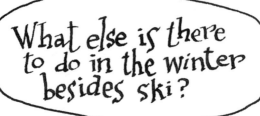

What else is there to do in the winter besides ski?

I guess visitors hibernate in the winter, because I sure don't see many of them around the park. If you decide to leave your cave and venture into Yosemite during winter, you'll find an entirely different world from the one we have in summer. Not only does the tourist population drop, but so do the leaves on the trees, making it easier to spot the wildlife foraging in the valley. The sounds of waterfalls and rushing rivers are replaced with the soft hush of snowfall. This peacefulness has its reward: it's cheaper. Rooms are less expensive at the park hotels and easier to get, even on short notice.

The best things about winter in the park are all the special seasonal activities. From mid-November to March 31, Curry Village opens its outdoor ice rink. For $5 for adults and $4.50 for children under age twelve, you can enjoy the views of Half Dome and Glacier Point while skating under a starry sky, or sit beside a crackling fire drinking hot chocolate. Skate rentals are $2, and the starry sky is free. For more information, call (209) 372-8341.

Once the snow starts falling, kids of all ages think of one thing: play time! To get your dose of fun, head for the slippery slopes near Crane Flat Campground and the Tioga Road juncture, or just south of the park on Highway 41 at Goat Meadow in the Sierra National Forest. Both are great areas for sledding, tobogganing, and inner-tubing.

If you have a pair of snowshoes, you can hike around on your own on some snow-covered terrain, like that at Badger Pass, Crane Flat, and the Mariposa Big Trees. There are also ranger-led walks (snowshoes provided) departing every day of the winter from Badger Pass. For more information, call (209) 372-0265. Snowshoes and boots are available to rent at Badger Pass for $11.50 per day.

The Yosemite Association offers winter field seminars, allowing visitors to explore the history, geology, and ecology of the park. For schedules and reservations, call (209) 379-2321. Kids can take part in their own special program, the Junior Snow Rangers, which allows them to have fun with a variety of hands-on learning activities. Call (209) 372-0265 for details.

Some of you might prefer the warmth and comfort of a winter motor coach tour. In heated buses with large windows, you can take a two-hour tour of Yosemite Valley, which leaves several times daily from valley hotels. Prices are $16 for adults, $15 for seniors, and $8.50 for children ages five through twelve. Check with hotel tour desks for times and reservations, or call (209) 372-1240.

Where can we swim in the park?

Our streams and lakes may be a little on the chilly side, but after roaming around on a hot day, I wouldn't have it any other way. Before I tell you about some good swimming holes, you should learn a few precautions. Sometimes the water temperature is a little too refreshing; don't stay in too long, or else hypothermia becomes an issue. Currents are another potential danger, especially during spring runoff and near waterfalls and rapids. As thirsty as you may be, don't ever drink river or lake water. A little organism called *Giardia lamblia* sometimes hangs out in the water, and if it gets inside you, your vacation could be ruined by bloating, fatigue, and far too much time spent on the toilet.

YOSEMITE VALLEY

From mid to late summer, you'll find plenty of swimming holes along the Merced River's sandy beaches at the eastern end of the valley. You can take a dip in Mirror Lake before it dries up the summer, and in Tenaya Creek before fall turns it into Tenaya trickle.

It's either a bear in swimming gear or a rare mountain platypus.

SOUTH YOSEMITE

The South Fork of the Merced in Wawona is dotted with swimming holes and beaches. There are plenty of lakes in the region's high country, but you have to be an official member of the Polar Bear Club to swim in them. From the Merced Lake High Sierra Camp, you can take a dip in the swimming holes downstream and search for one of our natural waterslides.

NORTH YOSEMITE

The Hetch Hetchy Reservoir is a no-go for swimmers, but nearby there's some good summer and fall swimming in a few high country lakes, such as Eleanor, Laurel, and Vernon. Along the Tioga Road the best spot is Tenaya Lake, which has some sandy beaches on its eastern shore. Closer to Tuolumne Meadows, you'll probably need to show your Polar Bear Club membership card again, but there are plenty of places to swim along the river near the Tuolumne Meadows Campground and Lyell Canyon and in some fun lakes such as Elizabeth and Dog.

Just to let you know, none of these spots is a designated public swimming area, so you're in charge of your own safety. Hey, there are always the warm swimming pools at Yosemite Lodge, Curry Village, and the Wawona and Ahwahnee Hotels.

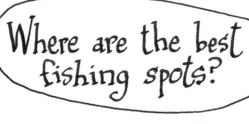

Where are the best fishing spots?

The fishing here is average, and I'm not just saying that to cut down on the competition. You can fish one hundred twenty-seven lakes and reservoirs year-round. If you want my advice, try some of the lakes off Tioga Road such as Lukens, Tenaya, and May Lakes, or some others near the High Sierra Camps. Around Tuolumne Meadows, take your best shot on Cathedral, Elizabeth, and Dog Lakes. Some people like to fish the Hetch Hetchy Reservoir and the rainbow trout fisheries on nearby Laurel and Vernon Lakes.

The fishing season for our rivers and streams runs from the last Saturday in April to November 15. We have a catch-and-release policy here, requiring barbless hooks and artificial flies and lures in Yosemite Valley. The western end of the valley along the Merced River provides some decent fishing. My favorite stretch is the year-round trout stream (designated "wild") near El Portal. Yosemite Creek and the Dana Fork of the Tuolumne River have been known to yield a fish or two; so has the South Fork of the Merced, where it winds through Wawona.

A valid California fishing license is required for anyone over age sixteen. You can purchase licenses good for one year for $25.70 (for California residents; out-of-staters will be charged more) at the Sports Shop in Yosemite Village, the Tuolumne Meadows Store, and the Wawona Store. You may also want to check out one-day fishing licenses. The daily limit is five fish per day and ten in possession. For special regulations on Yosemite Valley, check with the *Yosemite Guide* newspaper, visitor centers, or park information stations (see the telephone directory on pages 151–155).

Where can we learn to rock climb?

ROCK CLIMBER

When you see the sheer granite cliffs looming large over the valley, you'll wonder how anyone could ever climb these monsters and who would ever want to. Yosemite is actually one of the world's most popular rock climbing areas, attracting hundreds of climbers every year.

You can give the sport a try yourself; the Yosemite Mountaineering School is one of the best at teaching the craft of climbing. Classes are offered in Yosemite Valley during spring and fall and in Tuolumne Meadows during summer. Rock climbing takes skill and strength; proper training and conditioning are a must. Whatever you do, don't try scaling our peaks without proper instruction. The rates depend on the number of people in the class. For more information, call the Yosemite Mountaineering School at (209) 372-8344 in the spring and fall and at (209) 372-8435 in the summer.

Watching rock climbers has become a park attraction in its own right. Looking up at the wall of El Capitan or Half Dome, you might see a single tiny speck slowly making its way up the face. It sure isn't me you see up there; it's a person "free soloing" without the help of a climbing partner or rope. It's hard to imagine, but most of Yosemite's largest rock landmarks have been climbed in less than a day.

Anyone interested in...uh... rafting?

Can we go boating on the Merced River?

If you like the idea of floating downstream past breathtaking views of Yosemite Valley, then rafting the Merced is your ticket. In the summer, rental rafts with paddles and life jackets are available at Curry Village. Don't worry, you don't have to walk back; a tram picks you up and takes you back to Curry Village. The cost is $12.50 per person for all-day rentals, but it usually only takes three or four hours to float the entire stretch between the former Yosemite Valley Stables and Cathedral Beach. Due to dangerous rapids in other areas, this is the only section of the Merced open to rafters. You'll need at least two people but four maximum per boat. Just in case you rock the boat a little too much, it's a good idea to secure valuables in waterproof containers and tie coolers and other items to the raft.

Rafts, canoes, and kayaks can be used on the Merced without a permit. Life preservers, inner tubes, and air mattresses are allowed from Clark's Bridge at the Pine's Campground to the Cathedral Beach picnic area. Near Wawona, you can ride the South Fork of the Merced from 10 a.m. to 6 p.m. from Swinging Bridge to the Wawona Campground. From spring to midsummer, the heavy runoff swells the rivers and streams; that's when it's required to use U.S. Coast Guard–approved flotation devices. When it gets too dangerous, they close the Merced to all boating and swimming.

The thrill of white-water rafting can be experienced on an eighteen-mile guided river trip that tackles the rapids around the lower Merced River Canyon outside the park near El Portal. The cost is about $120 per person (including lunch). For more information, call Mariah Wilderness Expeditions, (800) 462-7424.

You can sail and float the waters of eight lakes in the park, but Tenaya Lake is the only one that's easily accessible. You'll have to lug your boat along wilderness trails to reach Merced, May, Benson, Tilden, Twin, Kibbie, and Thousand Islands Lakes. Motorboats are not allowed, and U.S. Coast Guard–approved flotation devices are required for each person on board.

Can we go horseback riding?

High in the saddle, you can get a unique perspective without ever breaking a sweat while riding the trails in the High Sierra.

The Wawona Stables offers summer tours around Wawona Meadow (two hours), up to Chilnualna Falls (four hours), and to Deer Camp (nine hours). Call (209) 375-6502 for more information.

From Tuolumne Stables, there are two-hour rides to Tuolumne View, four-hour rides to Tuolumne Fall, and nine-hour rides to Waterwheel Fall or Young Lakes. Call (209) 372-8427 for more information (summer only).

Costs (subject to change) are $35 for two hours, $45 for four hours, and $67 for all-day rides, western riding gear and helmets included. Children must be at least seven years old to ride.

You can also arrange to bring your own horse to Yosemite, where most of the designated trails are open to stock. Off-trail riding is prohibited, and regulations are pretty tight on animals brought into the park. Privately owned horses, mules, and burros can be kept overnight in the Wawona, Bridalveil Creek, Yosemite Creek, Tuolumne Meadows, and Hetch Hetchy campgrounds, or in the two park stables, by advance reservation and permit only. Call (209) 375-0265 for more information.

We packed our in-line skates and our skateboards. Is it okay to use them?

I've seen people breezing along the bike paths and paved roads on those in-line skates; it looks like a pretty fun way to get around. You just have to be extra careful of hikers and bikers using the same paths.

Skateboarders looking for good hills to cruise down will be out of luck in the valley: it's pretty flat, and it's not a good place to practice all those fancy tricks, like hopping over a deer or a tour kiosk. There are no regulations that say you can't use skates or skateboards in the park, but that will quickly change if rangers see any speed skaters or daredevils bothering other park visitors.

Can we play golf in Yosemite?

Golfers do have a place to go in Yosemite, and that doesn't mean teeing off the top of Half Dome for a longest-drive contest. The Wawona Hotel has a nine-hole, thirty-five-par golf course built in 1917 that's open from early April to mid-October, with lots of challenging roughs and water hazards. The first hole often has a few deer obstacles that you have to watch out for as well.

If golfing is not your thing, you can still take advantage of the scenic walk through the course's forests and meadows before it opens at 8 a.m. or after it closes at 5 or 7 p.m., depending on the season.

You can rent golf clubs and carts at the Wawona Golf Shop, and I recommend reserving a tee time. Prices are $13 for nine holes and $19.50 for a round of eighteen. Carts will cost you $11.50 for nine holes and $18.50 for the long haul. The Wawona Hotel also has an Autumn Golf Package. Call (209) 375-6572 for information and reservations.

SHOO!! SHOO!

GRRRRR

Never get between a bear and her clubs!

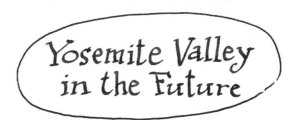

Yosemite Valley in the Future

The New Year's flood of 1997 began a natural process of change in Yosemite. It damaged rooms, campsites, and picnic areas for visitors and housing for those who work in the park. In summary, it sped up the process of reducing the impact of visitation on Yosemite Valley.

Now, what nature has started the National Park Service will carry out in the form of a plan, based on provisions in the 1980 General Management Plan (GMP) to remove unnecessary structures and restore recovered land to a more natural state, to relocate facilities out of sensitive or hazardous areas, and to reduce traffic congestion in Yosemite Valley.

In November 1997 the National Park Service issued their draft of Yosemite Valley Implementation Plan (VIP), which contains four alternatives, each with varying degrees of change and time frames But no matter which path is taken or how long it takes to go into effect, it will probably mean new ways for visitors to experience the valley in the future.

By the year 2001, a trip to Yosemite Valley may include some of the following elements:

⇨ Visitor arrival at a visitor facility at the western end of the valley, at a lodging or campground, or a gateway community. From each of these arrival points visitors would explore the valley either by guided walking tours, shuttle bus, valley floor tour, bicycle, or on foot.

⇨ Day-use visitors would arrive by regional transit bus or leave their cars in a staging area and use the valley connector shuttle, bicycle, or foot path to see the valley.

⇨ Visitor facilities would provide improved information, orientation, and wayfinding services for visitors.

⇨ Interpretive exhibits would be expanded and/or upgraded, and there would be both a human and natural history museum in the valley.

⇨ A new Native American Cultural Center for ceremonial use would be built.

⇨ New amphitheaters would provide space for expanded interpretive programs.

⇨ Park and concessionaire headquarters would be removed from Yosemite Valley and relocated outside the park's boundaries in El Portal.

⇨ 147 acres that are now developed or impacted would be restored to a more natural state, and other areas would be redesigned to improve visitor circulation or resource management of sensitive or hazardous areas.

⇨ There would be a slight reduction in campsites and lodging accommodations in the valley; work on the Yosemite Lodge may begin as early as October 1998.

These changes are estimated to take place over a five- to ten-year period.

Requests for more information on the implementation plan should be addressed to:

Superintendent
Attention: VIP Planning
Yosemite National Park
P.O. Box 577
Yosemite National Park, CA 95389
(209) 372-0265

or visit the Yosemite Valley Implementation Plan website at www.nps.gov/planning/yosemite/vip/.

Bruinhilda's Farewell

Whew! That was a lot of talking for a bear!

I hope I've answered all of your questions about Yosemite, and I hope that you've learned some inside information on ways to make your visit to the park more enjoyable.

The next part of this book is called the "Quick Reference" section. It's filled with lots of easy-to-find facts, forms, and information about the park. The subjects are in alphabetical order so you can quickly find what you need without having to thumb through the whole handbook. My favorite part of the section is the telephone directory, which gives you numbers for everything I talked about in the book.

Good hunting, and be sure to let us know if we need to change anything to improve future versions of this handbook. You can write to me or Susan and Phil Frank c/o Pomegranate, Box 6099, Rohnert Park, CA 94927.

Bye for now,

Bruinhilda

Quick Reference

1833 Yosemite Valley was first seen by Euro-Americans. While crossing the Sierra, the Joseph Walker party encountered a valley with "precipices more than a mile high" which were "impossible for a man to descend."

1851 The Mariposa Battalion under the command of Major James Savage became the first group of pioneers to enter Yosemite Valley. They were pursuing "intransigent" Indians.

1852 The Mariposa Grove of Giant Sequoias was discovered by a party of prospectors.

1855 The first tourist party visited Yosemite Valley with James Mason Hutchings as guide. Thomas Ayres, an artist with the group, made the first known sketches of Yosemite Valley.

1856 The first permanent structure, the Lower Hotel, was built in Yosemite Valley at the base of Sentinel Rock. The first trail into Yosemite Valley was completed by Milton and Houston Mann.

1859 The first photograph in Yosemite Valley was made by C. L. Weed. His subject was the Upper Hotel.

1864 Yosemite Valley and the Mariposa Big Trees were set aside by the federal government as the first state park in the world. Florence Hutchings was the first white child to be born in Yosemite Valley.

1866 Galen Clark was named the first Yosemite Guardian.

1868 John Muir made his first trip to Yosemite.

1871 The first ascent of Mt. Lyell, Yosemite's highest peak, was accomplished by J. B. Tileston on August 29.

1874 The first road into Yosemite Valley, the Coulterville Road, was completed. The Big Oak Flat Road was finished a month later.

1875 George Anderson made the first ascent of Half Dome before the installation of ropes or cables. The first public school was opened in Yosemite Valley.

1876 John Muir's first article on the devastation of the Sierra Nevada by sheep was published.

1878 The first public campgrounds were opened in Yosemite Valley by A. Harris near the site of the present-day Ahwahnee Hotel.

1890 Yosemite National Park established. The park did not include Yosemite Valley or the Mariposa Big Trees, but encompassed a large region around them.

1891 The first telephones were installed in Yosemite Valley.

1892 Trout were first planted in Yosemite waters by the California Fish and Game Commission.

1896 Firearms were prohibited from the park.

1898 The first civilian park ranger, Archie Leonard, was employed at Yosemite.

1900 The first automobile (a Locomobile) was driven into Yosemite by Oliver Lippincott and Edward C. Russell.

1907 The first railway line to Yosemite, the Yosemite Valley Railroad, began operation.

1913 Automobiles were "officially" admitted to Yosemite.

1915 First appropriation for the construction of the John Muir Trail approved.

1916 The National Park Service (NPS) was established. Washington B. Lewis was named the first NPS Superintendent of Yosemite.

1917 The first High Sierra Camp, Tuolumne Meadows Lodge, was installed.

1919 The first airplane, piloted by Lt. J. S. Krull, landed in Yosemite Valley on May 27.

1921 The first installations in the Yosemite Museum were completed.

1928 The Yosemite Museum opened to the public.

1934 The first water from the Hetch Hetchy Reservoir flowed into San Francisco Bay.

1935 Badger Pass Ski Area was developed.

1940 Ostrander Ski Hut was opened for winter use.

1946 The first ascent of the Lost Arrow Spire by four climbers was accomplished on September 2.

1949 The first use of a helicopter for rescue purposes was made at Benson Lake to fly an injured boy to safety.

1951 The first airplane planting of trout was done in Yosemite.

1954 Park visitation exceeded the one million level for the first time in history; 1,008,031 visitors were recorded.

1958 The first climb up the face of El Capitan was completed.

1961 Pioneer Yosemite History Center opened to the public.

1966 New Yosemite Valley Visitor Center built.

1967 For the first time over two million visitors were recorded.

1969 The "fire fall" from Glacier Point was discontinued. The famed "Wawona Tunnel Tree" toppled over from the weight of its winter snow load.

1970 The free shuttle bus system was initiated in Yosemite Valley.

1972   The first asphalt was removed from the parking lot in front of the Yosemite Valley Visitor Center. The area was converted to use as a pedestrian mall.

1974   Hang gliding was officially allowed from Glacier Point. One hundred seventy flights were made.

1976   The Tioga Road opened April 10, its earliest opening on record.

1980   The Yosemite General Management Plan was completed and approved. It was the first systematically developed, long-range planning document for the park.

1981   Captive-born Peregrine falcon chicks were successfully reared in a nest on El Capitan.

1983   The first ever prescribed burn was accomplished in the Mariposa Grove of Big Trees.

1984   Yosemite was named to the World Heritage List. The California Wilderness Bill designated 89% of the park as wilderness.

1986   California bighorn sheep were reintroduced into Yosemite.

1987   Park visitation exceeded three million for the first time: 3,266,342 visitors were recorded.

1990   Yosemite celebrated its hundredth birthday as a national park. Major forest fires raked the park during August.

1993   The Yosemite Concession Services Corp. (YCS) takes over from Yosemite Park & Curry Co. as concessionaire for the park's hotels and business operations.

1995   Park visitation exceeded four million for the first time: 4,101,928 visitors were recorded. The first woman to head a major national park, B. J. Griffin, was named superintendent of Yosemite in February. Beginning in March, the park was plagued with rockslides, flooding, and snowstorms that closed roads into the park. Overcrowding and traffic congestion in the summer caused the valley to be closed to cars for seven consecutive weekends. A government budget crunch shut down the park twice over Christmas and New Year's.

1997   The worst flooding to hit Yosemite Valley in more than a century closed the park from January 1 to March 14 and caused extensive damage to roads, utilities, housing, lodging, picnic areas, and campgrounds in the valley. The Yosemite Valley Stable was closed at the end of the summer season, and the draft Yosemite Valley Implementation Plan was issued for public comment. One of the primary goals of the plan is to reduce future crowding and traffic congestion in the valley as outlined in the 1980 General Management Plan.

Chronology from *The Complete Guide to Yosemite National Park* by Steven P. Medley. Used with the permission of the Yosemite Association.

FIELD SEMINARS

The Yosemite Field Seminar Program sponsored by the Yosemite Association (YA) offers classes geared to educate visitors of all experience levels on a wide range of topics, including botany, geology, ecology, ornithology, Native American culture, art, and photography.

There are outdoor seminars, many offered for college credit, that last from one to eight days. These are usually limited to groups of ten to fifteen people, and are offered in all areas of the park from February to November (weather permitting).

Most of the seminars' prices include reserved cabin rooms or free shared tent campsites. Campers need to bring their own tent, ground cloth, sleeping pad, sleeping bag, flashlight, cooking stove and fuel, food, and all personal gear. All campgrounds have cold running water and flush toilets, but no showers, electricity, or hook-ups. No pets are allowed.

Courses held at Crane Flat are hosted by the Yosemite Institute, a youth educational organization. This rustic campus includes dorm accommodations and showers, and breakfast and dinner are served family style. Lunches are provided on the trail.

For more information and a listing of current field seminars, call the YA office at (209) 379-2321 (e-mail: YOSE_Yosemite_Association@nps.gov).

INTERPRETIVE PROGRAMS

Many types of interpretive programs covering a wide range of subjects are offered both day and night in the park. Included are art classes, films, theater productions, and special ranger walks and talks about photography, geology, and the history of Yosemite. Actor Lee Stetson assumes the role of Yosemite's first naturalist, John Muir, as he leads a walk around the valley. Yosemite Valley offers the widest range of programs, but you can also attend a ranger-guided talk at the following locations: Wawona, the Mariposa Grove, Glacier Point, Tuolumne Meadows, Crane Flat, and Big Oak Flat. Check the *Yosemite Guide* newspaper for schedule and details, or call the Valley Visitor Center at (209) 372-0298 or 372-0299.

Yosemite Concession Services (YCS) also offers year-round interpretive programs on a wide range of subjects. For more information, call YCS at (209) 372-1001.

TEACHER WORKSHOPS AND CLASSROOM PROGRAMS

The National Park Service (NPS), in partnership with the Yosemite Institute, conducts workshops offering classroom teachers tools of environmental education about Yosemite and the Sierra. The workshops combine curriculum training with trips exploring park environments. Extended education credits are available through California State University at Fresno. A five-day workshop is offered in the summer, and weekend workshops are offered in the spring and fall. For more information and a registration packet, call the Yosemite Institute at (209) 379-9511.

Yosemite has a "Parks as Classrooms" program that offers ranger-led field trips around the park. Designed to fit within the California State curriculum, the programs emphasize the message of protection and preservation of natural and cultural resources. Class size is limited to thirty-five students, with two classes maximum per day. The cost of $35 includes instruction, supplies, and materials (park entrance fees are waived for educational visits). For more information, call (209) 375-9538.

ON-LINE INFORMATION SERVICES

You can browse through several different Yosemite web sites for park information and educational programs.

The official NPS Home Page (http://www.nps.gov/yose/) gives you all of the latest information about the park. You'll be able to look through a growing collection of Yosemite Notebooks that cover a large variety of Yosemite activities.

The Yosemite Association page, Yosemite Online (http://yosemite.org) gives you visitor information, a bookstore, a listing of outdoor classes, daily weather forecasts, a live camera view of Glacier Point, a 3-D Quicktime Video of Yosemite Valley, and membership information.

The Yosemite Fund Page (http://www.connect.net/yosemite/) often has park project updates, with photographs showing restoration work at Glacier Point and the rockfall at Happy Isles. Other features include "Wild Card," "Waterfalls!" and "Tips for Travelers," along with current donation information.

The Yosemite Concession Services website (yosemitepark.com) is the newest Yosemite online service. It features two hundred pages of information on lodging, shopping, dining, and park activities.

PROGRAMS AT LECONTE MEMORIAL

The LeConte Memorial Lodge (shuttle shop #12), Yosemite's first public visitor center, is run by the Sierra Club and offers a variety of evening environmental education programs geared for visitors, with special children's programs in the summer. Inside you'll find a children's corner, library, and exhibits. It's open 10 a.m. to 4 p.m., Wednesday through Sunday, May 1 to September 30. Evening programs are offered at 8 p.m., Friday through Sunday. Call (209) 372-4542 for more information.

YOSEMITE EDUCATIONAL EXHIBITS

American Indian Cultural Exhibit (shuttle stops #6 and #9) displays the cultural history of the native Miwok and Paiute people from 1850 to present. Open daily from 9 a.m. to 4:30 p.m.

The Yosemite Museum Fine Arts Gallery (shuttle stops #6 and #9) reveals the park as seen through the eyes of many great artists. Check gallery doors for hours of operation.

The Visitor Center Art Exhibit (shuttle stops #6 and #9) features artwork depicting various areas of Yosemite. Open daily from 9 a.m. to 5 p.m.

The Wilderness Center (shuttle stops #6, #9) provides essential information and tools for trip planning, camping techniques, and wilderness issues. Open daily from 7:30 a.m. to 7:30 p.m.

Happy Isles Nature Center (shuttle stop #16) includes natural history exhibits and a bookstore. Open daily from 10 a.m. to 4 p.m.

Pioneer Yosemite History Center (Wawona) offers self-guided tours of the Living History exhibit of historic Yosemite buildings, complete with volunteers dressed in period costume. Open summers only.

Mariposa Grove Museum (Mariposa Grove) has exhibits about the amazing giant sequoias. Open summers only.

Thomas Hill Art Studio (Wawona Hotel) presents tours of the artist's studio, where he worked from 1885 to 1908. Open summers only.

Tuolumne Meadows Visitor Center at Tuolumne Meadows is just south of Tioga Road and west of the gas station. Exhibits explain the Tuolumne Meadows region and Yosemite high country. Open summers only.

THINGS TO DO WITH KIDS:

The Yosemite Association has some great books for kids who want to explore the park. *The World of Small* comes with a magnifying lens to teach kids how "big" small things can become. *The Happy Camper Handbook* comes with a flashlight and rescue whistle, and introduces the family to all aspects of camping. To order books or receive a publications catalog, call (209) 379-2648.

The Nature Center at Happy Isles has wildlife exhibits, a children's corner, a display of Yosemite at night, and special children's books. Sign up for an Explorer Pack at Happy Isles or Tuolumne Meadows Visitor Center. The Nature Center is open daily from late spring until October at shuttle stop #16, or call (209) 372-0287.

Junior Ranger Programs are available year-round in Yosemite Valley, Wawona, and Tuolumne Meadows to kids ages eight through twelve, who can explore the mysteries of Yosemite while earning certificates and patches. Check the *Yosemite Guide*, the seasonal park newspaper, for details or call (209) 372-0265.

Visit the Village of the Ahwahnee located behind the Valley Visitor Center. It's a reconstructed Miwok-Paiute American Indian Village open spring to fall, with a self-guided walking tour. In summer you can see daily "living history" demonstrations of food preparation and hand crafts. Check the *Yosemite Guide* for details.

Step back in time at the Pioneer Yosemite History Center (open summer) near the Wawona Hotel. Park rangers and volunteers dress in period costume and give visitors a "living" history of the people and events that shaped Yosemite. Attractions include exhibits and rides in horse-drawn carriages, a working blacksmith shop, and the 126-year-old restored covered bridge that once stood over the Merced River. Self-guided or ranger-led tours are also available. Check the *Yosemite Guide* for details, or call (209) 375-9501.

Home Planet Hootenanny features the Recycled String Band singing and playing lively, environmentally oriented songs for summer visitors. "**Yosemite By Song and Story,**" playing at the Yosemite Theater, is another great show for the entire family. Check the *Yosemite Guide* for schedule.

The LeConte Memorial children's center offers special educational programs for kids during the summer. Call (209) 372-4542, or check the *Yosemite Guide*.

Daily nature walks led by rangers take visitors on easy one- to two-hour hikes. Check with any visitor center or the *Yosemite Guide* for details.

Evening campfire programs and performances are scheduled at various locations around the park from late June to early September, providing a memorable and entertaining way for families to spend their Yosemite vacations. Check the *Yosemite Guide* for times and locations.

Free art and photography classes are offered to adults and children ages ten and older, spring though fall, and during the Thanksgiving and Christmas holidays in Yosemite Valley. Reservations are accepted twenty-four hours in advance at the Art Activity Center, located at the east end of the Village Mall.

Year-round outdoor recreational activities abound for families. Whether you prefer walking, hiking, biking, horseback riding, rafting, sailing, skiing, snowboarding, snowshoeing, ice skating, or just playing in the snow, you can find it all in Yosemite. Refer to "Recreational Opportunities" on pages 95–122 for more information and details.

HISTORIC YOSEMITE PEOPLE

John Muir
John Muir is probably the most important individual in the history of Yosemite National Park. When the young Scotsman arrived in San Francisco in 1868, he asked directions to "anywhere that's wild." A few years later he was living in a self-built cabin on the banks of Yosemite Creek. Muir worked in Yosemite as a millworker and shepherd, but as he watched more and more settlers and visitors pour into the park and saw how they treated the landscape, he decided his most important job was to protect and preserve the land he came to love. For the remainder of his days, Muir traveled extensively through the Sierra Nevada, studying, documenting, and mapping the terrain and became a well-known Yosemite guide for many people, including Ralph Waldo Emerson and President Theodore Roosevelt. In 1889, Muir joined forces with magazine editor Robert Underwood Johnson, and together they lobbied for federal protection of the region. Their efforts were rewarded in 1890, when Congress set aside fifteen hundred acres as Yosemite National Park. Muir later became the first president of the Sierra Club, formed to secure additional preservation and protection for the Yosemite region. Muir died in 1914 at the age of seventy-six.

Chief Tenaya
When the first Euro-Americans came to Yosemite in 1851, Tenaya was the leader of the native Yosemite people. Revered as a legendary warrior and leader, Tenaya confronted the gold miners who were scouring the region for riches. He told them the Yosemite would remain peaceful as long as their lives in Yosemite remained undisturbed. Confrontations soon erupted, and in the spring of 1851, a volunteer army called the Mariposa Battalion stormed into the valley to drive Tenaya's tribe out of Yosemite. Tenaya was among a group rounded up and taken to a reservation in Fresno, but he soon escaped to his home in Yosemite. Battles between white settlers and the native people continued, and Tenaya fled with his band to Mono Lake to stay among their allies, the Paiute. In the summer of 1853, Chief Tenaya once again returned to the valley, but he was killed later that same year. A canyon, a lake, and other park features immortalize his name.

Galen Clark
For twenty-one years, Galen Clark worked to create and preserve Yosemite National Park. He is known as the pioneer of the home-

steading movement in the Sierra, where in 1856 he established 160 acres called Clark Station, predecessor of the Wawona Hotel. Clark successfully lobbied to get the Yosemite grant passed and signed by President Abraham Lincoln in 1864, making a small part of Yosemite a State Park. For his tireless efforts, Clark was appointed "Guardian of Yosemite," a role he honored by helping to protect the valley and sequoia groves and keeping roads and bridges in good repair to preserve access to the park. Clark died in 1910 just before his ninety-sixth birthday; he is buried in the Yosemite Valley Pioneer Cemetery under the sequoias he planted.

David and Jenny Curry
The Currys were pioneer innkeepers in Yosemite. In 1899 they established a small camp of seven tents and a dining area at the eastern end of the valley. During their first year of business, 292 people registered at the rustic resort, marking the beginning of Camp Curry and its famous tradition of campfire shows and talks in Yosemite. David Curry died in 1917, but "Mother" Curry lived until 1948, long enough to see her camp grow to include lodging for thirteen hundred guests. In 1925, the Curry Camping Company and the Yosemite National Park Company merged to form a single concession known as the Yosemite Park & Curry Company, which until 1993 operated all concessions in the park.

HISTORIC YOSEMITE PLACES

Ahwahnee Hotel (shuttle stop #4). Before the present hotel was opened in 1927, this was the site of an active stable business known as Kenneyville, which included horses, shops, barns, and houses. When automobile travel became popular, the stable was moved to its present location, and the old buildings were torn down. Between 1943 and 1945, the Ahwahnee was converted to a Navy convalescent hospital that served almost seven thousand patients.

Bridalveil Meadow (Southside Drive near Pohono Bridge). This is where the Mariposa Battalion, the first Euro-Americans to ever enter Yosemite Valley, camped in 1851. It is here that they proposed the name "Yosemite." President Teddy Roosevelt and John Muir camped here in 1903 to discuss the need to preserve Yosemite's wilderness areas.

The Famous Fire Fall (Glacier Point). It is believed that the idea for the first firefall came from James McCauley in 1871 or 1872. As a way of attracting visitors to the valley, burning embers were pushed over the edge of Glacier Point to create a stream of fire flowing down the cliff face. David Curry revitalized the tradition in 1899 during his tenure in the valley. Because of the growing negative impact of the event on Yosemite—including meadows trampled by the thousands of nightly spectators, not to mention the traffic jams—the decision was made on January 25, 1968, to discontinue the firefall.

Pioneer Cemetery (shuttle stop #3). From the 1870s to the 1950s, residents of Yosemite were buried in the cemetery located across the street from the Yosemite Museum in Yosemite Village. Walking through the cemetery, you'll see the graves of local native peoples Lucy and Sally Ann Castagnetto and of pioneer settlers and innkeepers, such as Galen Clark and James Mason Hutchings. Cemetery brochure guides are available at the Valley Visitor Center.

Sentinel Rock View (about 1.4 miles past El Capitan view). This was the site of Leidig's Hotel, which operated from 1869 to 1888; the site of Camp Ahwahnee from 1908 to 1915; and later, James McCauley's tollhouse, a collection booth for hikers and horseback riders as they started on the Four Mile Trail to Glacier Point.

Stoneman Meadow (near Curry Village, shuttle stop #4). On this site the State of California built a wooden hotel called the Stoneman House, which burned down in 1896. James Lamon, the first permanent pioneer resident of the valley, also built a cabin near here and planted two apple orchards. One of the orchard sites is now the Curry Village parking lot; the other is behind the stables in Yosemite Valley. Stoneman Meadow was also the site of a riot that took place in 1970, when young people clashed with staff over curfews, noise, and lifestyles.

Yosemite Falls (shuttle stop #7). Along the most eastern bank of Yosemite Creek, James Mason Hutchings built a lumber mill to help upgrade his hotel. John Muir ran the sawmill for Hutchings and constructed a cabin nearby for himself. Camp Yosemite, known as Camp Lost Arrow, stood near the base of the fall from 1901 to 1915.

Yosemite Lodge (shuttle stop #8). First built as Army headquarters for the park in 1906, the "lodge" included two large barracks, two bathhouses with lavatories, 156 tent frames, and a parade ground. The army left in 1914; in 1915 the facilities were converted for civilian visitors.

The Yosemite Association is a non-profit organization dedicated to the support of Yosemite National Park through a program of visitor services, publications, and membership activities. It receives no public funds or private endowments. For seventy years, the Association has provided the National Park Service with important financial assistance for research, scientific investigation, education, and environmental projects. Among its programs are the Art Activity Center, the Yosemite Theater interpretive programs, the Field Seminar program, the Ostrander Lake Ski Hut, and the Wilderness Center in Yosemite Valley.

Please enroll me in the Yosemite Association as a ...

❏ Regular Member – $25.00 ❏ Contributing Member – $50.00 ❏ Life Member – $500.00

❏ Supporting Member – $35.00 ❏ Centennial Member – $100.00 ❏ Participating Life Member – $1,000.00

❏ International Member – $35.00 (Residing outside USA)

❏ With spouse/partner – add $5.00

Name (please print): _____   Daytime Phone Number: _____

Address: _____   City: _____   State/Zip: _____

Enclosed is my check or money order for $ _____   or charge to my credit card

VISA / MasterCard / Am.Exp.: _____   Expiration Date: _____

Mail to:
Yosemite Association, Post Office Box 3240, El Portal, CA 95318   209/379-2646

For Office Use		
Paid:	Date:	Card #:	Gift:

139

The Yosemite Fund
Providing for Yosemite's Future

Yosemite's popularity, combined with severely limited funding, has taken a huge toll on park resources.

The Yosemite Fund was created in 1985 to provide funding for projects of lasting benefit to Yosemite National Park.

More than 30,000 Friends of Yosemite now share a belief that it is our responsibility to assist in further preserving this one-of-a-kind park.

Friends of Yosemite have already helped:

⇨ bring back the Bighorn sheep and Peregrine falcon
⇨ restore Stoneman Meadow
⇨ plant hundreds of oak seedlings and willow trees in Yosemite Valley
⇨ further protect giant sequoia trees
⇨ provide wheelchair access to visitor centers and vista points
⇨ many other projects of significant, long-term benefit to Yosemite

Please enclose your gift today to help Yosemite National Park.
Your gift is 100% tax deductible.

Yes! I want to help Yosemite!

Enclosed is a tax-deductible gift of:

$15 _____ $50 _____ $200 _____

$25 _____ $100 _____ $Other _____

As a donor of $25 or more you become a Friend of Yosemite. You receive a biannual newsletter, and your name is listed at the Honor Wall in Yosemite Valley.

Name _____

Address _____

City _____

State/Zip _____

The Yosemite Fund
(415) 434-1782
155 Montgomery Street, Suite 1104, San Francisco, CA 94104
or
P.O. Box 637, Yosemite, CA 95389

Ahwahnee: The Ahwahnechee people's name for both a large village near Yosemite Falls and for the greater Yosemite Valley. Lafayette Bunnell reported that the name meant deep, grassy valley, although this is unsubstantiated. Some linguists believe that "place of a gaping mouth" is a closer translation.

Big Oak Flat: A small town near Yosemite's northwestern boundary from which the Highway 120 route took its name. The massive oak (reportedly ten feet in diameter) which inspired the name is long since dead, the victim of miners' axes in the 1800s.

Chilnualna: This name, common in the Wawona area, is of unknown origin and meaning.

Clark: Yosemite Valley's first guardian in 1864 and the discoverer of the Mariposa Grove of Big Trees was Galen Clark. His name now graces a mountain, a mountain range, and other features in Yosemite.

Conness: A senator from California in the 1860s, John Conness introduced the bill in Congress that set aside Yosemite Valley and the Mariposa Big Trees as a state preserve. Mount Conness is an imposing peak on the park boundary north of Tioga Pass.

Crane Flat: Most probably named for a group of sandhill cranes encountered there by Lafayette Bunnell (John Muir also noted cranes at the location), although some assert the origin was a man named Crane who at one time resided at the spot.

Curry: David and Jennie "Mother" Curry established a small tent camp for the public in Yosemite Valley in 1899. It grew to become Camp Curry and later Curry Village. The merger of their operation with the Yosemite Park Company resulted in the Yosemite Park & Curry Co., a long-time concessionaire.

Dana: J. D. Whitney's California Geological Survey named a prominent peak east of Tuolumne Meadows for James Dwight Dana in 1863. Dana was a Yale professor and considered the foremost American geologist of his time.

El Capitan: This massive granite cliff was named by the Mariposa Battalion in 1851. It is the Spanish equivalent of the native Indian name *Too-tok-ah-noo-lah*, meaning "rock chief" or "captain." Other names assigned the rock at one time or another were Crane Mountain and Giant's Tower (Go Giants!).

El Portal: This Spanish term for gateway or entrance was used to name the terminus of the Yosemite Valley Railroad on the park's western doorstep. Now a small town on Highway 140, the site is slated to become the park's headquarters. Because of its searing summer heat, some have dubbed the place "Hell Portal."

Glen Aulin: At the behest of R. B. Marshall of the U.S. Geological Survey, James McCormick named this idyllic spot on the Tuolumne River in the early 1900s with the Gaelic phrase meaning "beautiful valley" or "glen." A High Sierra Camp was built there in 1927.

Half Dome: Credit the Mariposa Battalion with describing this split mountain as a half dome. Of all the landmarks in Yosemite, Half Dome has worn the most names over the years, among them Rock of Ages, North Dome, South Dome, Sentinel Dome, Tis-sa-ack, Cleft Rock, Goddess of Liberty, Mt. Abraham Lincoln, and Spirit of the Valley. Somehow a T-shirt imprinted with the phrase "I climbed on top of the Goddess of Liberty" wouldn't quite work.

Happy Isles: One of Yosemite Valley's early guardians named the three small islets on the Merced River for the emotions he enjoyed while exploring them ("no one can visit them without for the while forgetting the grinding strife of his world and being happy"). For years this was the site of a fish hatchery.

Hetch Hetchy: At one time a remarkably beautiful companion valley to Yosemite, Hetch Hetchy bears a Native American name of several meanings or interpretations, the most popular of which is a kind of grass or plant with edible seeds which abounded in the valley. Some believe *hetchy* means "tree," and that *hetch hetchy* is descriptive of two yellow pine trees that grew at the entrance to the place. Hetch Hetchy was dammed by the City of San Francisco in the 1920s.

Illilouette: This French-sounding name is actually an English translation (poor indeed!) of the Native American word *Too-lool-a-we-ack.* James Mason Hutchings opined that its meaning is "the place beyond which was the great rendezvous of the Yosemite Indians for hunting deer" (the great Miwok hunt club in the sky?).

Lembert: John Baptist Lembert was an early settler in the Tuolumne Meadows region. He built a cabin at the soda springs in Tuolumne, and his name is attached to the granite dome nearby.

Lyell: Yosemite's highest peak (13,114 feet) was named by the California Geological Survey in 1863 for Sir Charles Lyell, an eminent English geologist.

Mariposa: This Spanish word meaning "butterfly" was first applied to a land grant, later to the community, and then to the county. The sequoias at the south end of Yosemite were called the Mariposa Grove of Big Trees because Galen Clark discovered them in Mariposa County in 1857.

Merced: The Moraga party gave the Spanish name to this river when they crossed it in the San Joaquin Valley in 1806, five days after the feast day of Our Lady of Mercy. Originating in Yosemite's high country, the river was formally known as El Rio de Nuestra Señora de la Merced (River of Our Lady of Mercy). All other names utilizing Merced in Yosemite are derived from the river's name.

Mono: Derived from the Yokuts people's word *monoi* or *monai,* meaning "flies." At what is now known as Mono Lake, the resident natives harvested, ate, and traded millions of the pupae of flies, a favorite foodstuff of the native people of the region. The Shoshonean tribe grew to be known as the Mona or Mono tribe; many landmarks east of Yosemite bear this name.

Nevada: A name assigned to the waterfall on the Merced River by the Mariposa Battalion in 1851. The word signifies "snow" in Spanish; members of the battalion felt that the name was appropriate because the fall was so close to the Sierra Nevada and because the white, foaming water was reminiscent of a vast avalanche of snow.

Olmsted: A turnout from the Tioga Road near Tenaya Lake with a remarkable view, named for both Frederick Law Olmsted and his son, Frederick Law Olmsted Jr. The senior Olmsted was involved in the earliest development of the 1864 Yosemite grant and served as chairman of the first Board of Yosemite Valley Commissioners. His son worked as an National Park Service planner in Yosemite and had a position on the Yosemite Advisory Board.

Sierra Nevada: This is the Spanish phrase for "snowy mountain range." It was applied to California's greatest range of mountains by Father Pedro Font, who glimpsed it from near Antioch in 1776. Because the word *Sierra* implies a series of mountains, it is both grammatically and politically incorrect to use the term "Sierras." If you do, you will be castigated by self-righteous Yosemite word snobs.

Stoneman: A large hotel built by the State of California in 1885 once stood in the meadow just north of Curry Village. Known as the Stoneman House for then-Governor George Stoneman, it burned in 1896. The meadow and nearby bridge still bear the name.

Tenaya: The chief of the resident Indian tribe when the Mariposa Battalion entered Yosemite Valley in 1851 was named "Ten-ie-ya". The battalion first encountered the Native Americans living near the banks of a lake near Tuolumne Meadows, which they called Tenaya Lake.

Tioga: This is an Iroquois word meaning "where it forks," "swift current," or "gate." Miners at work on the Sierra Crest near Yosemite established the Tioga Mining District in 1878, apparently importing the name from Pennsylvania or New York.

Tuolumne: An Indian group residing in the Sierra foothills near Knights Ferry was known as "Taulamne," reportedly pronounced tu-ah-lum´-nē. The name was applied to the river originating in Yosemite and flowing through their territory. The pronunciation of the word in use today is tu-ah'-lum-ē.

Vogelsang: Colonel Benson, an American officer and acting superintendent of Yosemite National Park from 1905 to 1908, named a peak south of Tuolumne Meadows for either Alexander Vogelsang or his brother Charles Vogelsang, both of whom were affiliated with the California Department of Fish and Game. *Vogelsang* is German for "birdsong," an apt name for the site of the Vogelsang High Sierra Camp.

Wawona: Popular opinion holds that the word is the Native American name for "big tree." Native peoples viewed the big trees as sacred and called them *who-wo-nah.* The word is formed in imitation of the hooting of an owl that they believed to be the guardian spirit and deity of the sequoias.

White Wolf: A meadow on the route of the Tioga Road named by John Meyer who, while chasing the Indians came to the temporary camp of White Wolf, the band's chief.

Yosemite: This name was assigned to the world's most beautiful valley by the Mariposa Battalion in 1851. They believed that the Yosemite people (as they were apparently known) who resided there should have their true name perpetuated in the designation of the valley. The exact meaning of the name is disputed, but Lafayette Burnell, a member of the battalion, later wrote that the term signified "grizzly bear." He was informed that because grizzly bears frequented the territory occupied by the Yosemites and because the band was skilled at killing the bears, the name was taken as an appropriate one for the people.

Yosemite Place Names from *The Complete Guide to Yosemite National Park* by Steven P. Medley. Used with the permission of the Yosemite Association.

In 1980 the National Park Service (NPS) issued a management plan for Yosemite with the stated goals of restoring and preserving nature, as well as reducing traffic. Here's what's being done to meet those goals:

HABITAT CONSERVATION AND RESTORATION PROGRAMS

Along the bikeway between Yosemite Village and Yosemite Falls, plastic tubes protect black oak seedlings within roped-off areas. The goal is the restoration of a black oak woodland damaged by people and overgrown with conifers that competed with the oaks for space and light.

Some of the pioneer settlers and early park managers placed boulders and barriers in the Merced River, changing its flow. The National Park Service now has a restoration program designed to return the Merced and its ecosystem to a more natural state and has instigated a new catch-and-release regulation in Yosemite Valley to protect native rainbow trout.

Several of Yosemite's meadows are in the process of being restored. Volunteers have planted native vegetation, fenced meadows, installed boardwalks to channel foot traffic, and removed invasive non-native plant species.

When hikers step around muddy trails, they actually create new trails. In some meadows, four or more trails are cut, side by side. The NPS, with the help of the California Conservation Corps and other volunteers, has been filling and replanting the ruts in these trails, building raised causeways, and protecting the natural integrity of the meadows. Visitors can help by staying on established trails.

The 1995 High Sierra Camp season was canceled due to environmental concerns after a very wet winter. To reduce stress on the backcountry trails, Yosemite Concession Services and NPS initiated a High Sierra trail conservation program, which includes eliminating the transport of over twenty-one tons of specialty produce and linen into the back country each season. You'll still be able to eat generous portions of prepared meals at the High Sierra Camps, but without the heavier fruits and vegetables. You might want to bring your own 13.4-ounce travel sheet, since bed sheets are no longer provided.

Fire is an essential element in Yosemite's ecosystem. It reduces dead and down fuels, thins old vegetation, recycles nutrients, and enhances the health of our plants, many of which depend on fire for survival. Under certain safety conditions, the prescribed burning program uses controlled fires in areas of the park during early summer and mid-fall. Since 1970, prescribed burns have restored thirty-two thousand acres within the park; a little extra smoke in the air is worth it in the long run. For the same reason, in eighty-three percent of the park's wilderness, lightning-caused fires may be allowed to burn without intervention in areas full of dead and down fuel and where there's no threat to property or human lives.

To increase protection of river habitat and riparian resources, the Merced River has new rafting regulations. Rafters are asked to disembark only on sand or gravel bars. Fallen trees are no longer removed from the river, since they provide fish habitats and add nutrients to the aquatic food chain. The river will be closed when the water level is too high (seven feet or higher at Sentinel Bridge) or too low, when floating activities might disturb the river-bottom habitat.

PROTECTION OF ENDANGERED SPECIES AND ANIMAL REINTRODUCTION PROGRAMS

Peregrine falcons are making a comeback in Yosemite after being absent for many years. The NPS and the Santa Cruz Predatory Bird Research Group, with funding help from organizations and individuals, have helped increase the number of peregrines. Four nesting pairs with eight young were counted in 1995.

California bighorn sheep once roamed the Yosemite area, but they were eradicated by hunting, disease, and competition for food. Today the NPS, U.S. Forest Service, and California Department of Fish and Game have helped return the bighorns to the park's eastern edge. There are continuing studies to protect these animals from external threats such as disease from domestic sheep grazing near park boundaries.

WILDLIFE STUDIES

Mountain lions, peregrine falcons, goshawks, great gray owls, black bears, bats, and amphibians are being studied by the NPS in an effort to ensure their survival.

REDUCTION OF TRAFFIC AND POLLUTION

The YCS maintains a fleet of ten shuttle buses, including two emission-free electric test models, that shuttle visitors between nineteen points of interest in the valley. If the electric buses significantly help to reduce emissions in the valley, more will be added to the fleet until all park shuttles are powered by electricity or other alternative fuel sources.

RECYCLING IN YOSEMITE

Yosemite has one of the most extensive recycling programs in the national park system. Started in 1975, the program has won several national and state awards.

Glass, aluminum, paper, cardboard, and some plastics are accepted at the park's recycling centers at the Village Store and Curry Village. Refunds are also given for soft drink and beer containers at stores where the drinks are purchased.

Green recycling receptacles are located throughout park campgrounds, at picnic areas, and at many roadside turnouts.

Since 1988, there haven't been foam cups or containers in the park, due to the fact that they are non-biodegradable and a waste of costly fuels. Most of the hotel paper products and printed materials are made from recycled paper. Freon used in both park refrigeration systems and auto batteries are recycled.

PARTNERS IN PRESERVING THE PARK

The Yosemite Fund is a San Francisco-based, non-profit charitable organization that raises funds for preservation and restoration projects in the park. Since 1986, the fund has provided more than $7 million for more than one hundred Yosemite improvement programs. You can help efforts to preserve and restore Yosemite by ordering a distinctive four-color Yosemite Valley license plate. The plate is issued by the DMV for vehicles registered in California. For more information, contact the Yosemite Fund at (800) 4MY-PARK (469-7275) or (415) 434-1782.

Along with the Yosemite Fund, many active partners help raise money, sponsor educational programs, publish park information, and donate time and materials. These include the Yosemite Association, Yosemite Concession Services Corporation, Yosemite Institute, Sierra Club, Ansel Adams Gallery, San Francisco Conservation Corps, National Park Foundation, and Sousson Foundation, to name a few.

There are also scores of individuals who donate time and money, some of whom spend their vacation time working on park projects. These volunteers clean up rivers and trails, rehabilitate campgrounds, revegetate meadows and woodlands, uproot non-native plants, and act as campground hosts. You can join Yosemite's partners by joining the Yosemite Fund, the Sierra Club, or the Yosemite Association service project, or by volunteering for the NPS Volunteers in the Parks (VIP) Program. See the telephone listings on pages 151–155.

Campsite Reservation Request

Before mailing in this reservation form, call 800/426-PARK (7275) to reserve your campsite.

Please include middle initial in your name:

Name:

Address:

Zip: _____ Telephone: _____

No. of Persons: ___ Pet(s) ☐ Yes ☐ No

Important: Reservations may be made eight weeks in advance for Family Campsites.

National Park Service, P.O. Box 1600 Cumberland, MD 21502

If necessary, will you accept fewer nights? ☐ Yes ☐ No

Specific campsites cannot be reserved. Campsites are assigned upon arrival.

Be sure you complete all sections and enclose full payment. Incomplete or incorrect forms will be returned.

Type of camping equipment:

Check ✓ ♿

1	One tent or no equipment	17	
2	Two tents	18	
3	Large tent (over 9' x 12')	19	
4	Tent trailer	20	
5	Van or bus with side tent	21	
6	Pickup/camper thru 18'	22	
7	Pickup/camper thru 21'	23	
8	Motorhome thru 24'	24	
9	Motorhome thru 27'	25	
10	Motorhome over 27' ([ ] ft.)	26	
11	Trailer thru 15'	27	
12	Trailer thru 18'	28	
13	Trailer thru 21'	29	
14	Trailer thru 24'	30	
15	Trailer thru 27'	31	
16	Trailer over 27' ([ ] ft.)	32	

Golden Access or Golden Age Passport Serial No. if applicable:

Not Golden Eagle Passport or Park Pass.

Charges: The daily campsite charge is required for each period and/or campsite, up to the stay limit.

No. of nights _____ @ _____ * _____ =

No. of nights _____ @ _____ * _____ =

No. of nights _____ @ _____ * _____ =

*50% reduction for Golden Access or Golden Age passport

Total:

☐ Check/MO ☐ Discover ☐ MasterCard ☐ VISA

Card No.: _____ Exp: _____

Cardholder:

Telephone:

Signature:

Make payable to National Park Service and mail to: P.O. Box 1600, Cumberland, MD 21502

	First Choice:	**Second Choice:**	**Third Choice:**	Office Use
	Arrival Dates: Nights:	Arrival Dates: Nights:	Arrival Dates: Nights:	Nights:
Name of Park:				
Campground:				

Lodging

RESERVATIONS REQUEST FORM (*please print*)

Name

Phone

Address

City   State   Zip

Number in Party   Children   Ages

Preferred accommodation

Date of Arrival   Date of Departure

Number of Nights

2nd Choice, if preference is unavailable

Mail to:

Central Reservations
Yosemite Concession Services
5410 E. Home
Fresno, CA 93727

Number of cards you wish to purchase _____ x $26.81 each

Total Amount of Purchase $ _____

Credit Card Purchase: To purchase with a credit card, please complete the following:

Credit Card No. _____ Expiration Date _____

Circle Credit Card: Discover Card / Visa / MasterCard

Signature of Card Holder _____

OR

Make checks payable to: Yosemite Concession Services Corporation and mail to Yosemite Mail Order at the address below.

DO NOT SEND CASH. Please allow 4–6 weeks for delivery. For further mail order information and direct orders, Call: (209) 372-1354 or Fax: (209) 251-1501

All Orders: Daytime Phone _____

Yosemite Mail Order
5410 East Home Ave.
Fresno, CA 93727

Send merchandise to: (Please print clearly, as this will be your mailing label)

Name _____

Address _____

City _____ State _____ Zip Code _____

Now You Can
Save 10%
on groceries and gifts and
HELP
fund Yosemite Interpretive Programs.

THE YOSEMITE VALUE CARD

10% Discount in all YCS Gift, Apparel, Grocery, and Deli locations.

■

10% Discount on all-day bike rental.

■

Free Season Pass to Yosemite Lodge Pool.

■

Proceeds support the Yosemite Association and Yosemite Concession Services educational and interpretive programs.

For a contribution of $25 plus $1.81 tax, one card covers immediate family members and is good for one year from date of purchase.

Order a Yosemite Value Card by mail and receive a Yosemite Phone Card worth five minutes of phone calls FREE.

Remember: just as the park is always changing, so might its telephone numbers. Many of these phones are answered only in the summer months, and some are not staffed on a regular basis.

CAMPING AND BACKPACKING

Biospherics (campground reservations) 800/436-PARK (7275)
    International callers 301/722-1257
    TDD Service for the speech and hearing impaired . .888/530-9796
Big Oak Flat Information Station 209/379-1899
Crane Flat Grocery Store & Gas Station 209/379-2742
High Sierra Desk 209/253-5674
National Park Service Public Information Office 209/372-0265
Trail Conditions 209/372-0265
Tuolumne Meadows Campgrounds (summer) 209/372-4234
Tuolomne Meadows Ranger Station (summer) 209/372-0309
U.S. Forest Service Campgrounds
    Groveland Ranger Station 209/962-7825
    Mariposa Ranger Station .209/966-3638
    Mono Lake Ranger Station 619/647-3000
    Oakhurst Ranger Station .209/683-4665
Wawona Information Station 209/375-9501
Wawona Ranger Station 209/375-9520
Wilderness Permits 209/372-0740
Yosemite Association Field Seminars 209/379-2321
Yosemite Mountaineering School 209/372-8344
Yosemite Mountaineering School (summer) 209/372-8435
Yosemite Valley Ranger Station 209/372-0224
Yosemite Wilderness Center 209/372-0740

EDUCATIONAL EXHIBITS

Happy Isles Nature Center (summer) 209/372-0287
Indian Cultural Exhibit 209/372-0304
LeConte Memorial (summer) 209/372-4542
Mariposa Grove Museum (summer) 209/375-9501
Pioneer Yosemite History Center (summer) 209/375-9501
Thomas Hill Art Studio 209/375-1416
Tuolumne Meadows Visitor Center (summer) 209/372-0263
Valley Visitor Center Exhibits 209/372-0298/0299
Wilderness Center 209/372-0740
Yosemite Museum 209/372-0282

EDUCATIONAL PROGRAMS

LeConte Memorial Programs 209/372-4542
National Park Service Interpretive Programs . . .209/372-0298/0299
Parks As Classrooms 209/375-9538
Yosemite Association Field Seminars 209/379-2321
Yosemite Concession Services Programs 209/372-1001

Yosemite Education Office .209/375-9505
Yosemite Institute Programs 209/379-9511

GETTING AROUND

Badger Pass Ski Resort Conditions 209/372-1000
High Sierra Tour Desk 209/253-5674
Hikers' Bus, Glacier Point .209/372-1240
Hikers' Bus, Tuolumne 209/372-8441
Horseback tours 209/372-8384
Road and weather conditions (24-hour) 209/372-0200
Road and weather information (Mon.–Fri.) 209/372-0265
Shuttle Bus Information 209/372-1240
Sightseeing Tours by Bus .209/372-1240
Tram Tours of Mariposa Grove 209/375-9501
Tram Tours of Yosemite Valley 209/372-1240
Yosemite Lodge Tour Desk 209/372-1240

GETTING THERE

AMTRAK 800/USA-RAIL (872-7245)
California National Parks .415/556-6030
California Parlor Car Tours 415/474-7500
Educational Fee Waivers .209/375-9527
Entrance Fees 209/372-0200
General Yosemite information (24-hour) 209/372-0200
Lodging Reservations 209/252-4848
National Park Service (recorded) 209/372-0200
National Park Service Public Information Office 209/372-0265
900 Information Service (daily 8 a.m.–4:30 p.m.)   900/454-YOSE (9673)
Preferred Bus Charters 707/585-9110
Road and weather conditions (24-hour) 209/372-0200
Road and weather information (Mon.–Fri.) 209/372-0265
Tower Bus Tours 800/587-9484
Train and bus information (toll-free) 800/872-7245
Train and bus information 209/454-2080
VIA Bus Services and Tours (From inside California)   .800/369-PARK
VIA Bus Services and Tours (From outside California) .209/384-1315
Yosemite Concession Services Park Information (24-hour) 209/372-1000

LODGING AND DINING INSIDE YOSEMITE PARK

TTY Service Lodging Reservations for the Speech and Hearing
  Impaired 209/255-8345
Yosemite Valley
  All Lodging Reservations (YCS) 209/252-4848
  Front Desk Information
    Ahwahnee Hotel 209/372-1406

Camp Curry 209/372-8333
Housekeeping Camp 209/372-8337
Yosemite Lodge 209/372-1274
Dining
Ahwahnee dinner reservations 209/372-1489

South Yosemite
Lodging
Redwood Guest Cottages 209/375-6666
Wawona Hotel 209/375-6556
Yosemite West Cottages 209/642-2211

North Yosemite
Lodging
Evergreen Lodge (summer) 209/379-2606
Tuolumne Meadows Lodge (summer) 209/252-4848
White Wolf Lodge (summer) 209/252-4848
Dining
Evergreen Lodge Dinner Reservations 209/379-2606
Tuolumne Lodge Dinner Reservations 209/372-1313
White Wolf Lodge Dinner Reservations 209/372-1316

LODGING AND DINING OUTSIDE YOSEMITE PARK
Lodging
Best Western Lakeview Lodge, Lee Vining 619/647-6543
                                                    800/528-1234
Buck Meadows Lodge, Buck Meadows 209/962-4922
Cedar Lodge, El Portal .209/379-2612
Holiday Inn Express, Mariposa 209/966-4288
Holiday Inn Express, Oakhurst 209/642-2525
Mariposa Lodge, Mariposa 209/966-3607
Marriott's Tenaya Lodge, Fish Camp 209/683-6555
Mother Lode Lodge, Mariposa 209/966-2521
Narrow Gauge Inn, Fish Camp 209/683-7720
Oakhurst Lodge, Oakhurst 209/683-4417
Shilo Inn, Oakhurst 209/683-3555
Tioga Pass Resort 209/372-4471
Yosemite Gateway Best Western, Oakhurst 209/683-2378
Yosemite Redbud Lodge, El Portal 209/379-2301
Yosemite View Lodge, El Portal 209/379-2681
                                                    800/321-5261
Yosemite Westgate Motel, Buck Meadows 209/962-5281
Dining
Buck Meadows Lodge, Buck Meadows 209/962-5281
Cedar Lodge Restaurant 209/379-2612
Coffee Express, Groveland 209/962-7393

Happy Burger, Mariposa 209/966-2719
Hotel Charlotte, Groveland 209/962-6455
Narrow Gauge Inn, Fish Camp 209/683-6446
Nicely's, Lee Vining 619/647-6477
Tioga Pass Resort Dinner Reservations 209/372-4471
Yosemite View Lodge Restaurant 209/379-2681
800/321-5261

ONLINE INFORMATION SERVICES
National Park Service Home Page . . . . . . .http://www.nps.gov/yose/
Yosemite Area Transportation Information . . .http://www.yosemite.com
Yosemite Association e-mail . .YOSE_Yosemite_Association@nps.gov
Yosemite Association "Yosemite Online" . . . . . . .http://yosemite.org
Yosemite Concession Services . . . . . . .http://www.yosemitepark.com
Yosemite Fund Page . . . . .http://www.connect.net/yosemite/

PARK ATTRACTIONS
Ansel Adams Gallery .209/372-4413
Big Oak Flat Information Station 209/379-1899
Photo Walks 209/372-1240
Pioneer Yosemite History Center (summer) 209/375-9501
Ranger-led Walks 209/372-0265
Tuolumne Meadows Visitor Center 209/372-0263
Wawona Information Center (summer) 209/375-9501
Yosemite Bookstore .209/379-2648
Yosemite Museum 209/372-0282
Yosemite Valley Visitor Center 209/372-0299

PRESERVING YOSEMITE
Ansel Adams Gallery .209/372-4413
Sierra Club (LeConte Memorial) 209/372-4542
Volunteers In the Parks Program (VIP) 209/379-1850
Yosemite Association .209/379-2646
Yosemite Concession Services Corporation 209/372-1001
Yosemite Fund 800/4MY-PARK (469-7275); 415/434-1782
Yosemite Institute 209/379-9511

RECREATIONAL OPPORTUNITIES
Badger Pass Ski Resort (Recorded conditions) 209/372-1000
Badger Pass Cross-Country Ski School 209/372-8444
Badger Pass Downhill Ski School 209/372-8430
Bike Rentals (Curry Village) 209/372-8319
Bike Rentals (Yosemite Lodge) 209/372-1208
Glacier Point Ski Hut Reservations 209/372-8444
Golfing, Wawona 209/375-6572
Horseback riding, Tuolumne 209/372-8427

Horseback riding, Wawona 209/375-6502
Horses in Yosemite 209/375-0265
Ice Skating (Curry Village) .209/372-8341
Mariah Wilderness Expeditions, El Portal 800/462-7424
Ostrander Ski Hut Reservations 209/372-0740
Raft Rentals (Curry Village) .209/372-8341
Rock Climbing (spring & fall) 209/372-8344
Rock Climbing (summer) 209/372-8435
Snowshoe Walks, ranger-led 209/372-0265
Yosemite Association Field Seminars 209/379-2321
Yosemite Mountaineering School, Yosemite Valley 209/372-8344
Yosemite Mountaineering School, Tuolumne
  Meadows (summer) 209/372-8435

SPECIAL SEASONAL EVENTS IN YOSEMITE
Bracebridge Dinner (Ahwahnee) 209/252-4848
Chef's Holidays (Ahwahnee) 209/252-4848
Vintner's Holidays (Ahwahnee) 209/252-4848

SPECIAL VISITOR SERVICES
Golden Access Passports 209/372-0298, 0299
Sign Language Interpreter .209/372-0298
TTY Service for the Speech and Hearing Impaired
  (voice only) 209/372-0467
TTY Service for the Speech and Hearing Impaired 209/372-4726
Yosemite Medical Clinic Wheelchairs 209/372-4637
Yosemite Value Card 209/372-1354

THINGS TO DO WITH KIDS
Happy Isles Nature Center .209/372-0287
Indian Village of the Ahwahnee 209/372-0304
Junior Ranger Program 209/372-0265
LeConte Memorial Programs 209/372-4542
Pioneer Yosemite History Center 209/375-9501
Yosemite Bookstore 209/379-2648

WHERE CAN I FIND...?
Car repair and service 209/372-8320
Car towing service (24-hour) 209/372-1001
Dental Clinic 209/372-4200
Lost and Found 209/379-1001
Medical Clinic 209/372-4637
National Park Service Human Resources 209/379-1805
Yosemite Association Office 209/379-2646
Yosemite Concession Services Personnel Office 209/372-1000
Yosemite Volunteer Office .209/372-1850

	Jan	Feb	Mar	Apr	May	June	July	Aug	Sept	Oct	Nov	Dec
*Rainfall (ins.)	6.2	6.1	5.2	3.0	1.3	0.7	0.4	0.3	0.9	2.1	5.5	5.6
Max. Temp. °F	49	55	59	65	73	82	90	90	87	74	58	48
Min. Temp. °F	26	28	31	35	42	48	54	53	47	39	31	26

*37.2 inches annually

	January	April	July	October
Hours of Sunshine per day	3:57	7:38	9:34	6:45
Chances of a Sunny day	39%	70%	97%	81%
Afternoon Temperatures °F	48°	66°	90°	75°
Relative Humidity	86%	69%	50%	64%
Chances of a Dry Day	74%	80%	97%	94%
Snowfall	25.4"	4.5"	–	0.2"

High-country conditions are significantly cooler and much snowier during the winter months.

MATERIALS AND SERVICES FOR INTERNATIONAL VISITORS:

The "One Day In Yosemite" video in the Valley Visitor Center and the Yosemite Valley Audio Guide are both available in four foreign languages: French, German, Spanish, and Japanese. Many of the brochures about Yosemite are in the same four languages, and the Yosemite Association sells translated picture guides. Some park employees can act as translators, but only in emergencies.

THE YOSEMITE VALUE CARD ($25 PER YEAR):

Proceeds support evening Yosemite Concession Services (YCS) interpretive programs and the free art classes at the Yosemite Art Activity Center. Call (209) 372-1354 to order your card, or mail in the request card on page 150. The cards are also sold at the grocery store in Yosemite Valley. The card allows ten percent discounts at all YCS gift, apparel, grocery, and deli park locations; it's good for an all-day bike rental; and it includes a season pass to the Yosemite Lodge pool.

FACILITIES AND SERVICES FOR VISITORS WITH PHYSICAL DISABILITIES:

Golden Access Passes are available for visitors with disabilities, allowing free park entrance and discounted camping fees. Call the Visitor Center at (209) 372-0298 or 372-0299.

For visitors with mobility disabilities, the Valley Visitor Center provides a pass that allows driving access on the Happy Isles Loop and to Mirror Lake Meadow at 15 MPH, with emergency flashers on.

Visitors unable to board the Mariposa Tram Tour can drive behind a tram while they listen to a free audio tape of the tour in their car.

All buildings in the park have handicap access. Most of the valley campgrounds and four of the valley hikes are accessible with assistance. Check the *Yosemite Guide* for details.

Many of the visitor activities, like the art classes, ranger-guided walks, and the photo and John Muir walks, are wheelchair accessible. Check the *Yosemite Guide* for details.

Visitors with temporary disabilities are not entitled to a Golden Access Pass, but they can use temporary placards that allow use of places marked for disabled parking.

The Yosemite Medical Clinic also rents wheelchairs. Call (209) 372-4637 for details.

The park has at least one sign language interpreter during the summer months to assist hearing-impaired visitors. The "One Day In Yosemite" video and the orientation slide show in the Visitor Center are both captioned. To make arrangements for an interpreter, call the Visitor Center at (209) 372-0298, and check the *Yosemite Guide*.

The Yosemite Association (YA) offers a free field seminar designed for visitors with wheelchairs, as well as one for the hearing-impaired. Call the YA seminar office at (209) 379-2321 for details.

Mark Wellman, a former Yosemite park ranger, became the first paraplegic to climb El Capitan in 1989. In 1991, he and his climbing partner, Mike Corbett, climbed Half Dome. Now visitors can relive those famous climbs with Corbett at his evening program, "Courageous Climbers." Check the *Yosemite Guide* for details.

SPECIAL SERVICES AND DISCOUNTS FOR OLDER PERSONS:
All U. S. Citizens and legal residents age sixty-two and older can purchase a Golden Age Pass for a one-time fee of $10 from any of the park entrance stations. These passes provide discounts at all specified park facilities and tours.

Older persons with limited mobility can use parking places marked for disabled parking by obtaining temporary placards at the Valley Visitor Center.

WHERE CAN I FIND A GAS STATION?

Year-round stations are located in Wawona in the south part of the park and in Crane Flat in the north portion of the park. Tuolumne Meadows also has a station, but it is open only in the summer.

WHERE CAN I FIND A TOWING AND REPAIR SERVICE FOR MY CAR?

For towing services anywhere in the park, call (209) 372-1001, twenty-four hours a day. For repairs and service, call (209) 372-8320.

WHERE CAN I BUY PROPANE OR DIESEL FUEL?

You can buy propane in the valley (call 209/372-1001 for location) or at Wawona year round and at Tuolumne Meadows in the summer. Diesel fuel can be purchased at Crane Flat and Wawona.

WHERE CAN I FIND PUBLIC RESTROOMS? A PUBLIC SHOWER? A PUBLIC LAUNDROMAT? STORAGE LOCKERS?

Public restrooms are open at the following locations in the valley: near the parking lot for Yosemite Falls, across the street from Yosemite Lodge; behind the Valley Visitor Center; near the parking lot at the east end of Yosemite Village; at the Happy Isles Nature Center; near the Glacier Point parking lot; and at various locations along the backcountry trails.

You'll find public showers at Curry Village (all year) and Tuolumne Meadows Lodge (summer, very restricted hours). Remember, there are no public showers in Wawona. There's a laundromat at the Housekeeping Camp (spring through autumn). You'll find coin-operated public lockers at Curry Village on the west side of the registration office.

WHERE CAN I FIND A POST OFFICE? A BANK?

The park's main post office is open year-round in Yosemite Village. There's also a small year-round post office at Yosemite Lodge and the Wawona Store. Seasonal post offices operate at Curry Village and Tuolumne Meadows. There is no full-service bank in the park, but there's a Bank of America Versateller ATM and a cashier's office located in Yosemite Village next to the Village Store (shuttle bus stops #3 and #10, six buildings [200 yards] to the left as one leaves the Visitor Center).

WHERE CAN I CASH A CHECK, GET A CASH ADVANCE, OR HAVE FOREIGN CURRENCY EXCHANGED?

You can cash a personal check at the cashier's office located just beyond the Village Store with the following stipulations: picture ID and major credit card or check guarantee required; no two-party checks; $5 fee; $100 limit per day.

Guests of park lodging facilities may cash checks at front desks. You may cash one check for $50 or less per day without being charged a fee. Cash advances against credit cards (Visa, Mastercard, and Discover) are handled on a prorated fee basis. Foreign currency exchanges are not available in the park.

WHERE CAN I FIND THE LOST & FOUND OFFICE?

The Lost & Found office has moved to El Portal. It's best to call them at (209) 379-1001.

WHERE CAN I FIND A PHOTOCOPY MACHINE? SEND OR RECEIVE A FAX? GET A MESSAGE TO A FRIEND IN THE PARK?

You can find a photocopy machine at the Yosemite Lodge, the Ahwahnee Hotel, Curry Village, and the Yosemite Concession Services general office in Yosemite Village. A fax can be sent and received through the main post office in Yosemite Village or the front desks of the Yosemite Lodge, Curry Village, and the Ahwahnee Hotel. The National Park Service doesn't usually deliver messages to visitors in the park unless there's a real emergency. Call (209) 372-0265 in case of emergency.

WHERE CAN I GET A GOLDEN EAGLE PASS OR A GOLDEN AGE PASS?

The Golden Eagle Passes (good for all National Parks for one year from date of purchase) can only be purchased from rangers at park entrance stations. The cost is $50 annually. A pass good just for Yosemite will cost you $20 for one week and $40 for one year. Golden Age Passes, lifetime passes to all National Parks, can also only be purchased at park entrance stations and now require a one-time fee of $10 when issued to qualifying senior citizens (U.S. citizens or legal residents age 62 or older).

WHERE CAN I GET A JOB IN YOSEMITE? WHERE CAN I VOLUNTEER TO WORK IN THE PARK?

The National Park Service (NPS) has long lead-times for hiring. Contact the human resources office at (209) 379-1805. The Yosemite Concession Services (YCS) also has a personnel office located in the YCS General Office Building located at the opposite end of the Yosemite Village Mall from the Valley Visitor Center. The closest shuttle bus stops are #3 and #10, or contact the office at (209) 372-1000.

There are a number of ways to be a volunteer in Yosemite National Park. There's the campground host program, the V.I.P. (Volunteers in the Park) program, and the Student Intern Program. For more information, contact the Park's Volunteer Office at (209) 379-1850.

WHERE CAN I FIND THE SUPERINTENDENT'S OFFICE? THE CHIEF RANGER'S OFFICE?

To find the Superintendent's office, go out the front of the Visitor's Center, then turn right to the two-story Administration Building, a stone lower structure and a wooden upper structure. You'll find the office on the ground floor. The Chief Ranger is on the second floor of the same building.

WHERE CAN I FIND THE YOSEMITE INSTITUTE OFFICE?

Walk out in front of the Valley Visitor Center to the bike path near the bus stops, and turn right. Continue along the path past the first road crossing with a small bicycle stop sign. At the second road crossing with a small stop sign, turn right into the housing area. The Yosemite Institute office is the second house on the right with a sign in front.

WHERE CAN I FIND THE YOSEMITE ASSOCIATION OFFICE?

It has moved to the train station building near the post office in downtown El Portal. The telephone number is (209) 379-2646.

WHERE CAN I FIND THE U.S. DISTRICT COURT/MAGISTRATE'S OFFICE?

Walk out in front of the Visitor Center and immediately turn right down the path that goes past the Yosemite Museum building. Turn right on the first road, and go to the first stop sign. Turn right up the road that climbs the hill. At the top of the hill, a sign directs you to the left and the U.S. District Court.

If you're driving from the post office and visitor parking area, turn left as you leave the parking lot. Go uphill into the residential area. Follow the road to the top of the hill. There a sign indicates a right turn to the U.S. District Court.

WHERE CAN I FIND THE JAIL?

Make sure that you have approved business at the Law Enforcement Office before you go. Exit from the front of the Visitor's Center and immediately turn right down the path that goes past the Yosemite Museum building. Turn right up the road just beyond the Museum, and go up the road to the NPS maintenance yard/parking area. Follow the fire lane to the back of this area and to the large concrete building housing the NPS Firehouse. A door immediately to the right of the large Firehouse garage doors is marked "Law Enforcement Office"; go to the second floor.

CLOTHES
Sturdy hiking boots
Thick hiking socks
Lightweight liner socks
Long underwear
Fleece pants and sweatshirt
Rain-resistant jacket and pants
Warm hat and gloves
Oversocks and gaiters
Set of extra clothes
UV protection sunglasses

EQUIPMENT
Rain-resistant sleeping bag and pad
Backpacking tent and stakes
Frame backpack
Flashlight/headlamp
Water bottle
Backpacking stove and fuel
Cooking pot, cup, and utensils
Lighter or waterproof matches
Compass, map, pocket knife, and watch
Water purification device
Lightweight rope for hanging food
Bear-resistant canisters

SUPPLIES
Sunscreen, insect repellent, lip balm
Small first-aid kit with blister kit
Toilet items
Food

Wilderness permits can be obtained in person at the Wilderness Center in Yosemite Valley or at one of the stations listed below. At least fifty percent of each trailhead quota is available up to one day in advance, on a first-come, first-served basis. If you plan a Saturday start date, have a large group, and/or plan to use popular trailheads such as those in the Tuolumne Meadows area or to Little Yosemite Valley, Half Dome, or Merced Lake, you probably should make a reservation or pick up your permit a day in advance, early in the day, to assure trailhead access. Permits for the trail to Half Dome are only issued at the Yosemite Valley Permit Station, and you can count on a long line each morning.

Reservations for summer trips may be made by mail between March 1 and May 31. Send a letter that includes the dates you plan to enter and exit the wilderness, the specific trailheads where you plan to start and end, your principal destination, number of people in your group, and number of stock or pack animals, if appropriate. Be sure to include alternative dates and/or trailheads in case your first choice is not available. Mail reservation requests to Wilderness Reservations, Wilderness Center, P.O. Box 545, Yosemite, CA 95389. Be sure to include a $3 processing fee per person, and make your check payable to the Yosemite Association. Requests will be processed twenty-four weeks in advance of the first day of your trip. To reserve by phone, call (209) 372-0740, or complete the task in person at one of the following locations:

Wilderness Center
Yosemite Valley
(209) 372-0740

Wawona Information Station
(209) 375-9501

Big Oak Flat Information Station
(209) 379-1899

Tuolumne Meadows Ranger Station (summer only)
(209) 372-0309

THE LEGEND OF HALF DOME
In the days of the bird and animal people, one man traveled to Mono Lake to marry Tesaiyac. On their way back to Yosemite, she said she wanted to return to her home. They quarreled, and Tesaiyac started running back to Mono lake. With her husband in pursuit, she flung the basket she was carrying at him, and it became Basket Dome. Then she threw a baby cradle, where the Royal Arches are today. Because anger had been brought into Yosemite, the couple were turned to stone. He became North Dome and she, Half Dome, where you can still see the trail of her tears on the granite face, the same tears that formed Mirror Lake. Some say you can see the image of Tesaiyac in the vertical face of Half Dome.

THE LEGEND OF TULTAKANA
Long ago, two bear cubs living in the valley went swimming in the river. After they were done, they climbed to the top of a huge boulder to dry in the sun. They fell asleep and slumbered through many moons, and while they slept the boulder rose slowly to the heavens, until their faces scraped against the moon. The bird and animal people tried to bring the cubs down, but all failed. Along came Tultakana, a measuring worm, who was able to inch his way up the boulder and carry the cubs back down. In honor of the rescue, the boulder was named "Tultakana". Today it's known as El Capitan.

THE LEGEND OF U-WU-LIN, THE GIANT OF AH-WAH'-NEE
When the first bird and animal people inhabited the Valley of Ah-wah'-nee, it was a time of plenty, and they lived well. Then a great cannibal giant, U-wu-lin, appeared in the north and began to eat the people. The bird and animal people tried in every way to kill the giant, but nothing they could do would hurt him. Their arrows glanced from his body, and their spears were broken against his huge sides. The giant's heart was located in a tiny spot in his heel, and it was his only point of weakness. The bird and animal people, however, did not know where to find it. They asked Fly, who had a terrible bite, if he might help.

Fly went out to search for the giant and found him asleep; he began biting the giant everywhere. The giant gave no indication that he was aware of Fly until his heel was bitten; then he kicked his massive leg. Fly then knew he had found the giant's weak spot, and he returned to the bird and animal people to announce his exciting discovery.

The people decided to make a large number of long, sharply pointed stakes, which they placed all along the trail traveled by the giant. When the giant came down the trail, one of the awls pierced the heart in his foot, and he died immediately. In this way, peace was restored to the Valley of Ah-wah'-nee.

Excerpted with permission from *Legends of the Yosemite Miwok,* published by the Yosemite Association, 1993

Further Reading

Many of the following books may be purchased from the Yosemite Bookstore, which has sales facilities at Visitor Centers throughout the park. Call or write to place your order or to request a publications catalog:

Yosemite Bookstore
PO Box 230
El Portal, CA 95318
(209) 379-2648

- *Birds of Yosemite and the East Slope,* by David Gaines, illustrated by Keith F. Hansen. Lee Vining, California: Artemisia Press, 1992 (revised).

- *Complete Guidebook to Yosemite National Park, The,* by Steven P. Medley. Yosemite National Park: Yosemite Association, 1994.

- *Discovering Sierra Birds,* by Edward C. Beedy and Stephen L. Granholm, illustrated by Keith Hansen, John Petersen, and Tad Theimer. Yosemite Natural History Association and Sequoia Natural History Association, 1985.

- *Discovering Sierra Mammals,* by Russell K. Grater, illustrated by Tom A. Blaue. Yosemite Natural History Association and Sequoia Natural History Association, 1978.

- *Domes, Cliffs, and Waterfalls: A Brief Geology of Yosemite Valley,* by William R. Jones. Yosemite National Park: Yosemite Association, 1990.

- *Draft Yosemite Valley Implementation Plan and Supplemental Environmental Impact Statement,* produced by the United States Department of the Interior, National Park Service, Yosemite National Park, California, 1997.

- *Easy Day Hikes in Yosemite,* by Deborah J. Durkee, illustrated by Michael Elsohn Ross. Yosemite National Park: Yosemite Association, 1985.

- *50 Best Short Hikes in Yosemite and Sequoia/Kings Canyon,* by John Krist. Berkeley, California: Wilderness Press, 1993.

- *Gilbert Stanley Underwood: His Rustic, Art Deco, and Federal Architecture,* by Joyce Zaitlin, A.I.A. Malibu, California: Pangloss Press, 1989.

- *Handbook of Yosemite National Park,* compiled and edited by Ansel F. Hall. New York and London: G. P. Putnam's Sons, 1921.

- *Legends of the Yosemite Miwok,* compiled by Frank La Pena, Craig D. Bates, and Steven P. Medley, illustrated by Harry Fonseca. Yosemite National Park: Yosemite Association, 1993 (revised).

- *One Hundred Years in Yosemite,* by Carl Parcher Russell. Yosemite National Park: Yosemite Association, 1992.

- *Place Names of the High Sierra,* by Francis Farquhar. San Francisco: Sierra Club, 1926.

- *Sequoias of Yosemite National Park, The,* by H. Thomas Harvey. Yosemite National Park: Yosemite Association, 1978.

- *Wild Heritage: Threatened and Endangered Animals in the Golden State,* by Peter Steinhart. California Department of Fish and Game, California Academy of Sciences, and Sierra Club Books, 1990.

- *Yosemite: A Guide to Yosemite National Park,* produced by the Division of Publications, National Park Service. Washington, D.C.: U.S. Department of the Interior, 1990.

- *Yosemite As We Saw It: A Centennial Collection of Early Writings and Art,* by David Robertson, assisted by Henry Berrey. Yosemite National Park: Yosemite Association, 1990.

- *Yosemite National Park: A Natural History Guide to Yosemite and Its Trails,* by Jeffrey P. Schaffer. Berkeley: Wilderness Press, 1989.

- *Yosemite Road Guide,* by Richard P. Ditton and Donald E. McHenry. Yosemite National Park: Yosemite Association, 1989 (revised).

- *Yosemite: Saga of a Century,* edited by Jack Gyer. Oakhurst, California: The Sierra Star Press, 1965.

- *Yosemite Trout Fishing Guide,* by Steve Beck. Portland, Oregon: Frank Amato Publications, Inc., 1995.

- *Yosemite Valley: Secret Places & Magic Moments,* by Phil Arnot. San Carlos, California: Wide World Publishing/Tetra, 1992.

- *Yosemite Wildflower Trails,* by Dana C. Morgenson. Yosemite National Park: Yosemite Association, 1975.

- *Yosemite's Historic Wawona,* by Shirley Sargent. Yosemite, California: Flying Spur Press, 1979.

- *Yosemite Place Names,* by Peter Browning. Lafayette, California: Great West Books, 1988.

- *Yosemite's Yesterdays,* by Hank Johnston. Yosemite, California: Flying Spur Press, 1989.

Index

. many of her childhood weekends camping in the
nd fishing California rivers and lakes with her fami-
first grizzly bear on the Katmai Peninsula in Alaska
d spent more enjoyable hours waiting for fish to bite her
ctually catching them. After earning a degree in European
om the University of California, Berkeley, she taught in
sota and California before starting a career in communica-
. In 1990 she founded a media and marketing consulting com-
ny, working with a variety of clients throughout the San Francisco
ay Area.

About the Illustrator

Cartoonist Phil Frank's daily cartoon strip, "Farley," has been keeping
a finger on the pulse of the San Francisco Bay Area for more than ten
years, ever since Phil decided to leave national syndication to focus
his considerable talents on issues closer to home. The strip is dearly
loved and followed daily by a local cadre of fans. Indeed, "Farley"
has become one of San Francisco's most recognized and reliable landmarks.

Susan and Phil started their life together on a houseboat in Sausalito,
California. This led to their first book collaboration, a children's book
about living on the water. Both avid history buffs, they moved from
ship to shore about ten years ago. At present they maintain a 1914
Craftsman-style home in Sausalito, from which they venture into the
national parks and other wilderness areas in search of inspiration for
new books. They have two grown children, two grandchildren, two
Maltese-cross dogs, and two cats.